READING GROUP CHOICES
2013

*Selections for lively
book discussions*

READING
GROUP
Choices

ISBN 978-0-9759742-8-5

For further information, contact:
Reading Group Choices
532 Cross Creek Court
Chester, MD 21619
Toll-free: 1-866-643-6883
info@ReadingGroupChoices.com
ReadingGroupChoices.com

Welcome to READING GROUP Choices

The benefits of reading are undeniable. Researchers tell us that reading improves vocabulary, heightens world views, fosters empathy, and preserves memory and reasoning. All of this is true. But there is so much more to it than that. A great book is transformative, changing us forever not only intellectually but emotionally. The right novel takes us somewhere; maybe somewhere far away, maybe somewhere deep within ourselves. How often we find our minds returning to our favorite characters, drawing power from their experiences and insight into our own minds. I relish the moment when I am no longer seeing words on a page but instead *feeling* each moment as scenes unfold through the eyes of the characters. There is truly nothing like a great book to illuminate our lives.

To watch a person read is to see them transfixed in a world of their own; sitting in their favorite chair, eyes downcast, completely absorbed by the words on the page. This is where the fun of a book club comes in. A great book group discussion blows apart the walls that divide one reader from another. Here we can outwardly express our thoughts and feelings about a book. We can learn about the perceptions of others, and we can challenge our own ideas! Book clubs connect us with other people in a way that is filled with both meaning and fun. Many book clubs liven things up with good food, wine, and even theme meetings. There is no wrong way to bring people together to discuss a book.

This season we are pleased to present an outstanding collection to our readers. There is, literally, something for everyone. I would personally like to thank the team at **Reading Group Choices** for giving me the opportunity to act as the new *Literary Director* this year. It is an honor to work with such a wonderful group of people, all of whom are dedicated to Barbara Mead's dream of providing a fantastic literary resource for book clubs and individuals. Further, we would like to thank our friends in the book community as well as our publishing partners for all of their kind support.

Thank you for keeping the joy of reading alive!

NEELY KENNEDY
Literary Director

Book Group Favorites

Early in 2012, we asked thousands of book groups to tell us what books they read and discussed during 2011 that they enjoyed most. The top ten titles were:

1. *The Help* by Kathryn Stockett (Berkley Trade)

2. *Cutting for Stone* by Abraham Verghese (Vintage)

3. *The Immortal Life of Henrietta Lacks* by Rebecca Skloot (Broadway)

4. *Room* by Emma Donoghue (Back Bay Books)

5. *Still Alice* by Lisa Genova (Gallery)

6. *Sarah's Key* by Tatiana de Rosnay (St. Martin's Griffin)

7. *Major Pettigrew's Last Stand* by Helen Simonson (Random House Trade Paperbacks)

8. *The Paris Wife* by Paula McLain (Ballantine)

9. *The Book Thief* by Marcus Zusak (Alfred A. Knopf)

10. *The Hunger Games* by Suzanne Collins (Scholastic Press)

Contents

THE ABSOLUTIST
By John Boyne

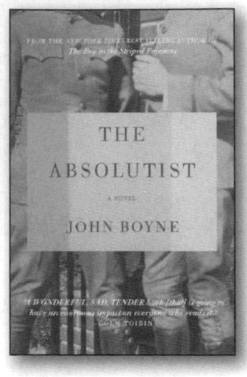

It is September 1919: twenty-one-year-old Tristan Sadler takes a train from London to Norwich to deliver a package of letters to the sister of Will Bancroft, the man he fought alongside during the Great War.

But the letters are not the real reason for Tristan's visit. He can no longer keep a secret and has finally found the courage to unburden himself of it. As Tristan recounts the horrific details of what to him became a senseless war, he also speaks of his friendship with Will—from their first meeting on the training grounds at Aldershot to their farewell in the trenches of northern France. The intensity of their bond brought Tristan happiness and self-discovery as well as confusion and unbearable pain.

The Absolutist is a masterful tale of passion, jealousy, heroism, and betrayal set in one of the most gruesome trenches of France during World War I. This novel will keep readers on the edge of their seats until its most extraordinary and unexpected conclusion, and will stay with them long after they've turned the last page.

"Powerful, poignant and beautifully written. This will become a classic war novel." —The Bookseller

"A novel of immeasurable sadness, in a league with Graham Greene's The End of the Affair. *John Boyne is very, very good at portraying the destructive power of a painfully kept secret."* —**John Irving**

About the Author: **John Boyne** was born in Dublin, Ireland, in 1971. He is the author of nine novels (seven for adults and two for children), including *The Boy in the Striped Pajamas*, which was made into an award-winning film. The novel also won two Irish Book Awards, was short-listed for the British Book Award, reached the top of *The New York Times* Best Sellers list, and has sold more than five million copies. His novels are published in forty-five languages. He lives in Dublin.

July 2012 | Trade Paperback | Fiction | 320 pp | $16.95 | ISBN 9781590515525
Other Press | otherpress.com | johnboyne.com
Also available as: eBook

CONVERSATION STARTERS

1. When Tristan first enters the Cantwell Inn, Mrs. Cantwell's son, David, presents the question of morality and describes the incident that happens in room four as "a personal indiscretion." Which characters does Boyne present as judges of morality in *The Absolutist?* How does Tristan's complete avoidance of their judgments define his character both negatively and positively?

2. In solitary confinement, Will makes it clear to Tristan what he dislikes about him and what makes them different. Tristan's silent compliance with the injustice of the military system and his insistence that their intimate moments hold some greater meaning come to repulse Will. Yet when Will removes his blindfold, his reaction suggests a kind of heartbreak. How do you read Will's reaction?

3. In the novel's carefully crafted structure, relationships and events build upon one another to culminate in an emotionally complex ending. What implications can we draw from Tristan's description of his father as a butcher? What parallels are being made and how do they help us understand Tristan's relationship with his father and with violence?

4. Tristan's internal conflicts with his family, with Marian, and with Will build in suspense. By not directly identifying Tristan's sexual orientation until later in the novel, Boyne allows room for a larger question of identity to develop. Consider Marian's position within her family and her community, David's ignorant desire to join the military, and Sergeant Clayton's development into a war fiend. How do these individual situations broaden Boyne's theme of troubled self-identity?

5. Tristan confides to Marian that he never took another lover after Will. This choice does not seem to be solely out of respect for the love he had for Will. Why else might Tristan insist on spending his remaining days alone?

6. In old age, Tristan reveals his plan to commit suicide and leave behind the story he has just told, accepting that this will ruin his reputation and cause him to be considered the greatest feather man of them all. How do you interpret Boyne's final treatment of Tristan's cowardice and self-image?

7. Tristan joins the firing squad on an angry impulse. Later he admits to Marian that he helped murder Will because he couldn't have him. Considering Will's reasons for being disappointed in Tristan, what is the irony of Tristan's action? What is implied when Tristan's own death approaches?

ALEPH
By Paulo Coelho

In his most personal novel to date, internationally bestselling author Paulo Coelho returns with a remarkable journey of self-discovery. Like the main character in his much-beloved *The Alchemist*, Paulo is facing a grave crisis of faith. As he seeks a path of spiritual renewal and growth, his only real option is to begin again—to travel, to experiment, to reconnect with people and the landscapes around him.

Setting off to Africa, and then to Europe and Asia via the Trans-Siberian railroad, he initiates a journey to revitalize his energy and passion. Even so, he never expects to meet Hilal. A gifted young violinist, she is the woman Paulo loved five hundred years before—and the woman he betrayed in an act of cowardice so far-reaching that it prevents him from finding real happiness in this life. Together they will initiate a mystical voyage through time and space, traveling a path that teaches love, forgiveness, and the courage to overcome life's inevitable challenges. Beautiful and inspiring, *Aleph* invites us to consider the meaning of our own personal journeys.

"A new tale of magical longing. . . . Masterful." —San Francisco Chronicle

"It's time for American readers to set out on a journey of discovery that will lead them to the works of this exceptional writer." —USA Today

ABOUT THE AUTHOR: The Brazilian author **Paulo Coelho** was born in 1947 in the city of Rio de Janeiro. Before dedicating his life completely to literature, he worked as theatre director and actor, lyricist and journalist.

June 2012 | Trade Paperback | Fiction | 288 pp | $15.00 | ISBN 9780307744579
Vintage | randomhouse.com | paulocoelho.com
Also available as: eBook and Audiobook

CONVERSATION STARTERS

1. *Aleph* is a novel full of rituals, starting with Paulo and J.'s opening invocation around the sacred oak. However, Paulo's reaction to them varies wildly; sometimes they frustrate him (the oak), sometimes he embraces them (the shaman's midnight chant on the edges of Lake Baikal), and other times he criticizes them for being empty (Hilal's offering at the church in Novosibirsk). Why do you think this is? Do you think this has to do with the rituals themselves or is Coelho trying to express something deeper about the nature and purpose of ritual? What value can ritual have in your own life?

2. Paulo frequently refers to Chinese bamboo after reading an article about its growth process: "Once the seed has been sown, you see nothing for about five years, apart from a tiny shoot. All the growth takes place underground, where a complex root system reaching upward and outward is being established. Then, at the end of the fifth year, the bamboo suddenly shoots up to a height of twenty-five meters." How does this function as an important metaphor for spiritual growth? What do you think are the best ways to build a "complex root system" of your own?

3. Coelho writes, "To live is to experience things, not sit around pondering the meaning of life" and offers examples of people who have experienced revelations in various ways. Do you agree? What people or writings are you familiar with that support (or disprove) his point of view?

4. What images, memories, and emotions most powerfully capture the mystery and the magic of the Aleph that Paulo and Hilal experience on the train? How do they affect them each as individuals? In what ways does it change and deepen their relationship?

5. What role does Yao serve in Paulo's quest? Are there similarities between Yao, Paulo, and the answers they seek?

6. Were you familiar with the concept of past lives before reading *Aleph*? Is it necessary to believe in past lives to grasp the book's message and meaning?

7. What do you think Coelho means when he writes, "Life is the train, not the station?" What about when he says, "What we call 'life' is a train with many carriages. Sometimes we're in one, sometimes we're in another, and sometimes we cross between them, when we dream or allow ourselves to be swept away by the extraordinary."

THE ANATOMIST'S APPRENTICE
A Dr. Thomas Silkstone Mystery

Tessa Harris

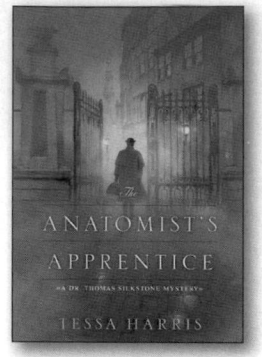

In the first in a stunning new mystery series set in eighteenth-century England, Tessa Harris introduces Dr. Thomas Silkstone, anatomist and pioneering forensic detective . . .

The death of Sir Edward Crick has unleashed a torrent of gossip through the seedy taverns and elegant ballrooms of Oxfordshire. Few mourn the dissolute young man—except his sister, the beautiful Lady Lydia Farrell. When her husband comes under suspicion of murder, she seeks expert help from Dr. Thomas Silkstone, a young anatomist from Philadelphia.

Thomas arrived in England to study under its foremost surgeon, where his unconventional methods only add to his outsider status. Against his better judgment he agrees to examine Sir Edward's corpse. But it is not only the dead, but also the living, to whom he must apply the keen blade of his intellect. And the deeper the doctor's investigations go, the greater the risk that he will be consigned to the ranks of the corpses he studies . . .

"*CSI meets* The Age of Reason *with a well-drawn, intriguing cast of characters, headed by the brilliant Dr. Thomas Silkstone. Full of twists and turns, Tessa Harris's debut mystery can confound the most adept reader. Vivid details pulled me right into the world of early forensic sleuthing. A page turner!*" —**Karen Harper**

About the Author: **Tessa Harris**, born in Lincolnshire, holds a history degree from Oxford University, and after four years of working with local newspapers she set her sights on women's magazines. She is regularly heard on local BBC radio and over the years has interviewed such people as Margaret Thatcher, Jeffrey Archer, Anthony Hopkins, Susan Hampshire, Alan Titchmarsh, Jackie Stewart, Boris Johnson, and Uri Geller. She lives in Berkshire with her husband and their two children.

January 2012 | Trade Paperback | Fiction | 304 pp | $15.00 | ISBN 9780758266989
Kensington Books | kensingtonbooks.com | tessaharrisauthor.com
Also available as: eBook and Audiobook

CONVERSATION STARTERS

1. Dr. Thomas Silkstone lived in England during the War of Independence (1775-1783). How did the attitude of the English change towards Americans during this period as reflected in the novel?

2. In chapter two we read that Mr. Smollett donated his remains for dissection. Would you donate your body to medical science?

3. Thomas is the voice of the Enlightenment in a turbulent age. What deeply embedded prejudices and superstitions does he battle against in the novel?

4. Captain Michael Farrell was a gambler and a rogue. But do you sympathize with him at any point in the novel?

5. Lady Lydia Farrell is not a conventional heroine. Her existence is dominated by over-bearing men. How far do you think this is a true reflection of a noblewoman's lot in Georgian society?

6. During an autopsy, Thomas muses on the exact location of the soul. It's a question that thinkers have been asking since time began. Has science brought us any closer to finding the answer?

7. There is a vast amount of historical detail in the narrative. Does this enhance or detract from the story?

8. The novel is written in the third person. Would the story have benefited if it were told through the eyes of Dr. Thomas Silkstone?

9. Discuss the treatment of servants in the Georgian household. What light does this shed on our relationships with employees today?

10. Should medicine be the sole preserve of highly qualified experts or is there room for alternative practioners like Hannah Lovelock?

11. Had Michael Farrell been sentenced for the murder of Lord Crick, an innocent man would have hanged. Can the death penalty ever be justified when there is any doubt around guilt?

12. How far did James Lavington's horrific injuries after his accident shape his character?

13. Discuss the mix of fact and fiction in the story. Does it help or hinder a novel when it is based on a true story?

ARCADIA

By Lauren Groff

In the fields of western New York State in the 1970s, a few dozen idealists set out to live off the land, founding what would become a commune centered on the grounds of a decaying mansion called Arcadia House. Arcadia's inhabitants include Handy, a musician and the group's charismatic leader; Astrid, a midwife; Abe, a master carpenter; Hannah, a baker and historian; and Abe and Hannah's only child, the book's protagonist, Bit, who is born soon after the commune is created. While Arcadia rises and falls, Bit, too, ages and changes. If he remains in love with the peaceful agrarian life in Arcadia and deeply attached to its residents—including Handy and Astrid's lithe and deeply troubled daughter, Helle—how can Bit become his own man? How will he make his way through life and the world outside of Arcadia where he must eventually live?

"Richly peopled and ambitious and oh, so lovely, Lauren Groff's Arcadia *is one of the most moving and satisfying novels I've read in a long time. It's not possible to write any better without showing off."* —**Richard Russo, author of the novel *That Old Cape Magic* and the Pulitzer Prize–winning *Empire Falls***

ABOUT THE AUTHOR: **Lauren Groff** is the author of *The New York Times* bestselling novel *The Monsters of Templeton* and the critically acclaimed short story collection *Delicate Edible Birds*. She has won Pushcart and PEN/O. Henry prizes and has been shortlisted for the Orange Prize for New Writers. Her stories have appeared in publications including *The New Yorker, The Atlantic, One Story*, and *Ploughshares*, and have been anthologized in *Best American Short Stories* 2007 and 2010, and *Best New American Voices* 2008. She lives in Gainesville, Florida, with her husband and two sons.

October 2012 | Trade Paperback | Fiction | 304 pp | $15.99 | ISBN 9781401341909
Voice | hyperionbooks.com | laurengroff.com
Also available as: eBook

CONVERSATION STARTERS

1. Thinking of Arcadia at its best moments, which of its values and tenets seem healthy and important for an individual? For a social group?

2. What's healthy or not for children being raised in an environment such as Arcadia? Consider the different ways Bit and Helle think about their upbringing.

3. Why is private property not allowed in Arcadia? What effect do you think this has on the identities of those living or raised there? What elements of your identity are independent of what you own?

4. Late in the story, there is a confrontation between Handy, Arcadia's founder, and Abe, one of its leaders. How are these two men different? In what ways are they successful or failed leaders? To what extent does someone's personal or private life affect his or her ability to lead?

5. Consider the long span of Hannah's life. What have been her strengths and weaknesses as a member of Arcadia?

6. Consider the various uses of pharmaceuticals and other drugs in the novel: the Trippies' permanent damage due to LSD; marijuana as recreation or economic crop; the medication that Hannah is on most of her adult life to adjust the "brain chemistry" that causes her depression. How do we determine which are healthy and which are not?

7. One of Bit's responses to his mother's deep depression is to decide he needs a Quest. Real or imagined, how might a Quest be psychologically important or effective as a response to emotional difficulty?

8. Consider the complex character that is Helle: her precocious behavior when young; the confrontation with Handy, her father; her disturbing sexual encounter in the woods; her vague, apologetic explanation to Bit, "I thought you knew who I was"; and her return and relationship much later with Bit, the birth of Grete, and her eventual disappearance. What do you understand about her nature and behavior?

9. Bit recalls how, as a boy, he made lists of beautiful things, a "litany" he would whisper to his mother to try to stir her out of depressive sleep. As an adult, in the midst of his troubles with his mother and wife, he does so again, this time for himself. Read his, and then try to make your own. Be specific to your personal experience. Then consider how such a gesture affects you and what role it might play in our everyday lives.

BELLA FORTUNA
By Rosanna Chiofalo

Valentina DeLuca has made hundreds of brides' dreams come true. At Sposa Rosa, the Astoria, New York, boutique where she, her sisters, and their mother design and sew couture knock-off gowns, she can find the perfect style for even the most demanding customer. Now, it's her turn. Valentina has loved Michael Carello ever since he rescued her from a cranky shopkeeper when she was ten years old. He's handsome, chivalrous, and loyal. And in a few weeks, she's going to marry him—in Venice.

But just when she thinks everything is falling into place, Valentina is forced to re-examine her life to see what truly makes her happy. And as she soon learns, in a place as magical as Venice, what seems like misfortune can turn out to be anything but, although who knows what may be waiting around the next corner?

"Sometimes tough, sometimes tender, always heartfelt and honest, Bella Fortuna *is a lively, finely-stitched tale of life and love, family and friendship, and a zest for cose Italiane!"* **—Peter Pezzelli, author of** *Villa Mirabella*

"Chiofalo's debut is an inspiring read about second chances with love after tremendous heartbreak." —RT Book Reviews

ABOUT THE AUTHOR: **Rosanna Chiofalo** is a first-generation Italian American whose parents emigrated from Sicily to New York in the early 1960s. After graduating with a BA in English from Stony Brook University, Rosanna knew she wanted to be around books and have a career in writing. For twenty years, she's worked as a Copywriter and Copy Director for several New York City publishing houses. Currently, she is hard at work writing her second novel.

September 2012 | Trade Paperback | Fiction | 368 pp | $15.00 | ISBN 9780758266538
Kensington Books | kensingtonbooks.com | rosannachiofalo.com
Also available as: eBook

CONVERSATION STARTERS

1. Do you feel that Valentina has truly been "cursed in love" as she proclaims in the opening chapter of *Bella Fortuna*? Do you feel that she's been unlucky in general in life?
2. How is Valentina different from her mother in her beliefs of the mighty malocchio or evil eye? How are they alike in their beliefs of good versus bad luck?
3. Do you agree with Aldo's assessment that Valentina has put Michael on such a high pedestal and that no one can live up to such high expectations? Does that make it easier to forgive Michael's transgressions later? Do you feel that Valentina's expectations of Michael are unrealistic?
4. Valentina is close to her family. But we also see she has a special relationship with her neighbors and the people in her neighborhood. Which is your favorite neighbor and why? Which is your least favorite neighbor and why? Do you feel that the neighbors are an extended family for Valentina?
5. What are Valentina's views on friendship with women? Do you feel that her views were shaped by Tracy's betrayal when they were in high school?
6. What does Valentina's wedding dress symbolize for her? What does the dress symbolize for her mother? Do you agree with Michael after he has walked in on her gown fitting that she should drop the shorter front hem of her dress? What do you think are his real motives in wanting a more traditional dress for Valentina?
7. Do you believe that Sonia, the teenage fortune-teller Olivia goes to see, truly has "the power"?
8. After Valentina returns to New York and visits Tracy's mother, she learns that Tracy seems to have changed her ways. Did you feel compassion for Tracy? Was it easier to understand her actions toward Valentina when they were in high school?
9. What did you think of Valentina's enormous gesture of giving Tracy's mother her wedding dress? Do you feel that her action has truly brought her peace?
10. How do Valentina's relationships with Michael and Stefano mirror her mother's relationships with her first love, Salvatore, and her husband, Nicola? How much did fate play a role in whom they fell in love with?
11. How have Olivia's views on bad luck changed toward the end of the novel? How have Valentina's changed?

THE BOOK OF TOMORROW

By Cecelia Ahern

Raised in the lap of luxury, spoiled and tempestuous sixteen-year-old Tamara Goodwin has never had to think about tomorrow. But when her world is irrevocably shaken by her father's self-imposed death, she and her mother are left drowning in debt and forced to move in with Tamara's peculiar aunt and uncle in a tiny countryside village.

Lonely and bored, Tamara's sole diversion is a traveling library. There she finds a large leather-bound book with a gold clasp and padlock, but no author name or title. Intrigued, she pries open the lock, and what she finds takes her breath away—for what's written inside is not only impossible and magical . . . it's her future.

"A veritable modern-day Gothic, Ahern's engrossing new novel is filled with family secrets, intrigue, and magic aplenty." —Booklist

"Ahern's tale-spinning prowess keeps the reader riveted." —Publishers Weekly

"[Ahern] takes a more gothic turn in her latest, recasting herself as a lost Brontë sister for the Facebook set. . . . Lovers of stories involving crumbling castles, nefarious family secrets . . . will be ecstatic." —Entertainment Weekly

ABOUT THE AUTHOR: At twenty-one, **Cecelia Ahern** wrote her first novel, *P.S. I Love You*, which became an international bestseller and was adapted into a major motion picture starring Hilary Swank. Her successive novels—*Love, Rosie; If You Could See Me Now; There's No Place Like Here; Thanks for the Memories; The Gift;* and *The Time of My Life*—were also international bestsellers, published in forty-six countries and selling more than 15 million copies collectively. The daughter of Ireland's former prime minister, Ahern lives in Dublin, Ireland.

July 2012 | Trade Paperback | Fiction | 336 pp | $14.99 | ISBN 9780061706318
William Morrow Paperbacks | harpercollins.com | cecelia-ahern.com
Also available as: eBook and Audiobook

CONVERSATION STARTERS

1. Moving to County Meath removes Tamara from her privileged, socially connected, overcommercialized life in Dublin. How does the teenager mature as a result of being away from her friends and the trappings of city life? Is the author of *The Book of Tomorrow* arguing for a more old-fashioned way of life, including books?

2. What were your first impressions of Sister Ignatius? Why does Sister Ignatius keep secrets? Is she a good friend to Tamara?

3. In chapter 15, Tamara has to make a tangible decision to go with or against the diary—reaching for either sugar or salt—and the chapter finishes open-ended on page 190. What did you expect her to do? Explain why.

4. The plot twists make *The Book of Tomorrow* an unexpected mystery. How does the diary serve as a map for Tamara to find answers? Is it always a faithful guide?

6. How do Tamara's friendships change over the course of the novel? In what ways do you think she outgrows her friends? How might her life have been different if they had kept in better touch?

7. How do you explain Tamara's relationship to Kilsaney Castle? Why do you think such a modern girl feels such a connection to an ancient ruin? Explain why she might feel so at home there.

8. How does Rosaleen's character develop over the course of the book? How did you feel about her at the beginning? Did your impressions change by the end? Were you surprised by what you discovered? What hints did the author provide in the story that may have pointed to the truth?

9. At the end of the novel Tamara discards the diary, saying, "I'll have to find my own way." Do you have faith that without the diary Tamara can try to live her tomorrows better? What, ultimately, has the diary taught her? Do you think she would have found her way without it?

10. Tamara says, "What if we knew what tomorrow would bring? Would we fix it? Could we?" How do you think Tamara answers this question throughout the novel? What is your answer?

11. Having a book of tomorrow is an intriguing and alluring idea. Do you think that you would enjoy having a diary predict the future's outcome? Would it take away the pleasure of the unknown or would it alleviate anxiety?

A BREATH OF EYRE

Eve Marie Mont

In this stunning, imaginative novel, Eve Marie Mont transports her modern-day heroine into the life of Jane Eyre to create a mesmerizing story of love, longing, and finding your place in the world . . .

Emma Townsend has always believed in stories—the ones she reads voraciously, and the ones she creates. Perhaps it's because she feels like an outsider at her exclusive prep school, or because her stepmother doesn't come close to filling the void left by her mother's death. And her only romantic prospect—apart from a crush on her English teacher—is Gray Newman, a long-time friend who just adds to Emma's confusion. But escape soon arrives in an old leather-bound copy of *Jane Eyre*.

Reading of Jane's isolation sparks a deep sense of kinship. Then fate takes things a leap further when a lightning storm catapults Emma right into Jane's body and her nineteenth-century world. As governess at Thornfield, Emma has a sense of belonging she's never known—and an attraction to the brooding Mr. Rochester. Now, moving between her two realities and uncovering secrets in both, Emma must decide whether her destiny lies in the pages of Jane's story, or in the unwritten chapters of her own.

"A rich, wonderful, smart adventure, steeped in romance. I fell into this book in the same way Emma falls into Jane Eyre *and I didn't want to fall back out again."* —**Lesley Livingston, author of *Once Every Never* and the *Wondrous Strange* trilogy**

"This richly satisfying tale of first and last love transcends its genre—not another breathless, fan-fiction take on a literary classic but an intertextual love letter with evocative settings and compassionately drawn characters, this trilogy opener offers affectionate insight into the gifts literature gives readers. A smart and rewarding ode to literature." —***Kirkus*, starred review**

About the Author: **Eve Marie Mont** lives with her husband, Ken, and her shelter dog, Maggie, in suburban Philadelphia, where she teaches high school English and creative writing. Her debut women's fiction novel, *Free to a Good Home*, was published by Berkley Books in 2010.

April 2012 | Trade Paperback | Fiction | 352 pp | $9.95 | ISBN 9780758269485
KTeen | kensingtonbooks.com | evemariemont.com
Also available as: eBook

CONVERSATION STARTERS

1. Why do you think Emma falls into *Jane Eyre* in particular? What does Jane's world offer her that her real world does not?

2. Several characters in both Emma's contemporary world and in the world of Jane Eyre are haunted by their pasts. How do guilt and regret affect each of them? What helps them to move on?

3. Both Emma and Michelle have lost their mothers. How does this bond help them connect? How does each girl deal with her grief?

4. Michelle does not know her father. How does this affect her sense of belonging and self-esteem?

5. What is the role of Michelle's Aunt Darlene in the narrative? How does Emma incorporate Darlene's voodoo beliefs into her own story?

6. Emma treasures her mother's dragonfly necklace. What does the dragonfly represent for her? Why do you think people cling so tightly to mementos with sentimental value?

7. Describe how Emma's relationship with her father changes throughout the story. What are the reasons for this change?

8. Many of the students in the novel have hobbies or passions such as horseback riding, writing, swimming, or music, but they are often forced to compete against others. Do you think the competition fostered in high schools is healthy or destructive? Why is it so important for teens to be good at something?

9. Why is Elise so hostile to Michelle and Emma? Do we ever find any reason to justify her actions, or is she just a villain?

10. How does the book convey the power of writing? What are some of the purposes writing serves in the book?

11. On the surface, Gray and Emma seem like opposites. Why do you think opposites often attract? What attracts Emma and Gray to each other?

12. What is the significance of water in the novel? Consider all the scenes in which water plays a role. How might this relate to Emma and Gray's growth as characters?

BRIDGE OF SCARLET LEAVES
Kristina McMorris

In this poignant and evocative novel by acclaimed author Kristina McMorris, a country is plunged into conflict and suspicion—forcing a young woman to find her place in a volatile world.

Los Angeles, 1941. Violinist Maddie Kern's life seemed destined to unfold with the predictable elegance of a Bach concerto. Then she fell in love with Lane Moritomo. Her brother's best friend, Lane is the handsome, ambitious son of Japanese immigrants. Maddie was prepared for disapproval from their families, but when Pearl Harbor is bombed the day after she and Lane elope, the full force of their decision becomes apparent. In the eyes of a fearful nation, Lane is no longer just an outsider, but an enemy.

When her husband is interned at a war relocation camp, Maddie follows, sacrificing her Juilliard ambitions. Behind barbed wire, tension simmers and the line between patriot and traitor blurs. As Maddie strives for the hard-won acceptance of her new family, Lane risks everything to prove his allegiance to America, at tremendous cost.

Skillfully capturing one of the most controversial episodes in recent American history, Kristina McMorris draws readers into a novel filled with triumphs and heartbreaking loss—an authentic, moving testament to love, forgiveness, and the enduring music of the human spirit.

*"Impeccably researched and beautifully written." —***Karen White,** *New York Times* **bestselling author of** *The Beach Trees*

"A sweeping yet intimate novel that will please both romantics and lovers of American history." —Kirkus Reviews

About the Author: **Kristina McMorris** is an award-winning author and graduate of Pepperdine University. A weekly TV host since age nine, including an Emmy Award-winning program, she lives in the Pacific Northwest with her husband and two sons. This is her second novel, following her widely praised debut, *Letters from Home.*

March 2012 | Trade Paperback | Fiction | 448 pp | $15.00 | ISBN 9780758246851
Kensington Books | kensingtonbooks.com | kristinamcmorris.com
Also available as: eBook

CONVERSATION STARTERS

1. The title *Bridge of Scarlet Leaves* was inspired by an ancient haiku. Describe the symbolism of leaves in the story and possible reasons they would be scarlet. What thoughts and/or emotions did the opening poem (by Deanna Nikaido) evoke both before and after you read the book?

2. In the 1940s, interracial marriage was illegal in more than thirty American states. Given expectations placed on Caucasian females during this conservative era, how do you feel about Maddie's hesitation early in her relationship with Lane? Would you have made the same daring choices that she did over the course of the war?

3. Several of the characters' lives often parallel throughout the story. Discuss such instances found in TJ's military training and tour, Lane's and Maddie's Manzanar experiences, Mrs. Duchovny's tragedy, and Dopey's assignment to the POW camp.

4. While working at the camo-net factory, Lane ponders the irony: "Here they were, unjustly imprisoned by their own country, contributing to the fight for freedom and democracy." In Lane's situation, would you have enlisted in the U.S. military? If drafted, would you have refused to serve?

5. A great number of historical facts and events, along with cultural tidbits, are woven through the pages. What was the most surprising or intriguing piece of information you learned?

6. Often the key to empathy lies in uncovering traumatic events that have shaped another person's life. Did your impression of Kumiko change once she revealed her past? Have you ever encountered a similar situation in which a discovery altered your perspective of a person?

7. At what point in the story do you believe Lane and Maddie's relationship truly became love? Do you believe Maddie regrets her choices? Reflecting on your own life, if you had foreseen the path ahead, would you have made the same decisions? Are you glad you didn't know beforehand?

8. In writing, Lane explains to Maddie that he had asked Dewey to throw away a previous letter. How do you think the discarded message differed from the one Lane ultimately sent?

9. Do you wish the story had ended differently for any of the characters? If so, how would that have affected the growth of the others? How do you feel about Dopey's decision after the war? Do you agree with Maddie's choice of placing a keepsake on the floating lantern?

BUDDHA IN THE ATTIC
By Julie Otsuka

A gorgeous novel by the celebrated author of *When the Emperor Was Divine* that tells the story of a group of young women brought from Japan to San Francisco as "picture brides" nearly a century ago. In eight unforgettable sections, *The Buddha in the Attic* traces the extraordinary lives of these women, from their arduous journeys by boat, to their arrival in San Francisco and their tremulous first nights as new wives; from their experiences raising children who would later reject their culture and language, to the deracinating arrival of war. Once again, Julie Otsuka has written a spellbinding novel about identity and loyalty, and what it means to be an American in uncertain times.

"Arresting and alluring. . . . A novel that feels expansive yet is a magical act of compression." —**Chicago Tribune**

"A stunning feat of empathetic imagination and emotional compression, capturing the experience of thousands of women." —**Vogue**

"A fascinating paradox: brief in span yet symphonic in scope, all-encompassing yet vivid in its specifics. Like a pointillist painting, it's composed of bright spots of color: vignettes that bring whole lives to light in a line or two, adding up to a vibrant group portrait." —**The Seattle Times**

About the Author: **Julie Otsuka** was born and raised in California. She is the author of the novel *When the Emperor Was Divine* and a recipient of the Asian American Literary Award, the American Library Association Alex Award, and a Guggenheim Fellowship. She lives in New York City.

March 2012 | Trade Paperback | Fiction | 144 pp | $13.95 | ISBN 9780307744425
Anchor | randomhouse.com | julieotsuka.com
Also available as: eBook and Audiobook

CONVERSATION STARTERS

1. Why is the novel called *The Buddha in the Attic*? To what does the title refer?
2. The novel opens with the women on the boat traveling from Japan to San Francisco. What does Otsuka tell us is "the first thing [they] did," and what does this suggest about the trajectories of their lives?
3. What are the women's expectations about America? Why are they convinced that "it was better to marry a stranger in America than grow old with a farmer from the village"?
4. Otsuka tells us that the last words spoken by the women's mothers still ring in their ears: "*You will see: women are weak, but mothers are strong.*" What does this mean, and how does the novel bear this out?
5. Why was the first word of English the women were taught "water"?
6. In the section entitled "Whites," Otsuka describes several acts of kindness and compassion on the part of the women's husbands. In what ways were the husbands useful to them or unexpectedly gentle with them in these early days?
7. What are the women's lives like in these early months in America? How do their experiences and challenges differ from what they had been led to expect? How are they perceived by their husbands? By their employers?
8. Later in this section, the women ask themselves, "*Is there any tribe more savage than the Americans?*" What occasions this question? What does the author think? What do you think?
9. Discuss the complexities and nuances of the relationship between the Japanese women and the white women. Was it strictly an employer/ employee relationship, or something more?
10. What is J-town? Why do the women choose J-town over any attempt to return home?
11. "One by one all the old words we had taught them began to disappear from their heads," Otsuka writes of the women's children. Discuss the significance of names and naming in *The Buddha in the Attic*. What does it mean for these children to reject their mother's language?
12. How do the dreams of the children differ from the dreams of their mothers?
13. Why do the women feel closer to their husbands than ever before in the section entitled "Traitors"?
14. Who narrates the novel's final section, "A Disappearance"? Why? What is the impact of this dramatic shift?

CAN I GET AN AMEN?

By Sarah Healy

When the last thing you want is the one thing you need, you've got to have a little faith . . .

Growing up, Ellen Carlisle was a Christian: she went to Jesus camp, downed stale Nilla wafers at Sunday school, and never, ever played with Ouija boards. Now, years later, when infertility prevents her from giving her ambitious attorney husband a family, she finds herself on the brink of divorce, unemployed, and living with her right-wing, Born-Again-Christian parents in her suburban New Jersey hometown. There the schools are private, the past is public, and blessings come in lump sums.

Then Ellen meets a man to whom she believes she can open her heart, and she begins to think that maybe it's true what they say, that everything happens for a reason. . . . Until all that was going well starts going very badly, and Ellen is finally forced to dig down deep to find her own brand of faith.

"Touching, funny, full of heart." —**Lisa Scottoline,** *New York Times* **bestselling author of** *Save Me*

"Funny, smart, wise, and refreshing. Can I Get An Amen? is the work of a great new talent and an obviously gifted writer." —**Valerie Frankel, author of** *Thin is the New Happy* **and** *Four of a Kind*

"An emotional and satisfying novel that's as tender as it is funny." —**Emily Giffin,** *New York Times* **bestselling author of** *Something Borrowed*

ABOUT THE AUTHOR: **Sarah Healy** lives with her husband and children in Vermont where she is at work on her second novel.

June 2012 | Trade Paperback | Fiction | 352 pp | $15.00 | ISBN 9780451236777
New American Library | us.penguingroup.com | sarah-healy.com
Also available as: eBook

CONVERSATION STARTERS

1. What was your general reaction to the novel? What did you like and not like about it?
2. Did you have any sympathy for Ellen's husband, Gary, who divorces her because she can't have a child? Do you think men and women tend to approach infertility in very different ways?
3. What do you think of the way Sarah Healy explores faith? Did the novel make you think about how faith can both bring families together and tear them apart?
4. Ellen's mother, Patty, accuses her of being close-minded about religion. In what ways might that be true? In what ways might the same criticism be lobbed back at Patty?
5. Ellen realizes that no one has ever asked her what religious beliefs she holds. Why don't we talk about our religious beliefs? Do we lose something by failing to?
6. Though Ellen seems ambivalent about Christianity, she always seems to turn to prayer during her most desperate times. Is it out of habit? Or do you think it signifies a deeper belief than she wants to admit?
7. It's ironic that Ellen's mother, Patty, makes Ellen's divorce and infertility public through a prayer request, yet Ellen's parents won't tell even their own children about their imminent bankruptcy. Have you ever found yourself in a similar situation, with someone accusing you of one thing while being guilty of it themselves?
8. In the novel, Sarah Healy gently bursts what some might consider religious fantasies—for example, the idea that "being Christian" and attending church will somehow protect us from bad things happening, and that the material goods we buy are "blessings" from God. Can you think of other current religious fictions?
9. Parker Kent is the villain of the novel, but Ellen has some sympathy for her at the end. Discuss the price that Parker pays to keep her marriage intact. What do you think Parker knew and didn't know about her father's behavior toward Jill during that visit to Nantucket? Do you think Parker's complicity back then influenced the kind of marriage she ended up having?
10. Did you find the end of the novel satisfying? If the book continued, what do you think would happen to the characters?
11. In the last line of the novel, Ellen states that she still doesn't know what she is, or how to define her beliefs. Can you sympathize with her uncertainty?

CATHERINE THE GREAT
By Robert K. Massie

The Pulitzer Prize–winning author of *Peter the Great*, *Nicholas and Alexandra*, and *The Romanovs* returns with another masterpiece of narrative biography, the extraordinary story of an obscure German princess who became one of the most remarkable, powerful, and captivating women in history. Born into a minor noble family, Catherine transformed herself into empress of Russia by sheer determination. For thirty-four years, the government, foreign policy, cultural development, and welfare of the Russian people were in her hands. She dealt with domestic rebellion, foreign wars, and the tidal wave of political change and violence churned up by the French Revolution. Catherine's family, friends, ministers, generals, lovers, and enemies—all are here, vividly brought to life. History offers few stories richer than that of Catherine the Great. In this book, an eternally fascinating woman is returned to life.

"*[A] tale of power, perseverance and passion . . . a great story in the hands of a master storyteller.*" —*The Wall Street Journal*

"*[A] compelling portrait not just of a Russian titan, but also of a flesh-and-blood woman.*" —*Newsweek*

ABOUT THE AUTHOR: **Robert K. Massie** was born in Lexington, Kentucky, and studied American history at Yale and European history at Oxford, which he attended as a Rhodes Scholar. He was president of the Authors Guild from 1987 to 1991. His previous books include *Nicholas and Alexandra*; *Peter the Great: His Life and World* (for which he won a Pulitzer Prize for biography); *The Romanovs: The Final Chapter*; *Dreadnought: Britain, Germany, and the Coming of the Great War*; and *Castles of Steel: Britain, Germany, and the Winning of the Great War at Sea.*

September 2012 | Trade Paperback | Nonfiction | 672 pp | $20.00 | ISBN 9780345408778
Random House Trade Paperbacks | randomhouse.com
Also available as: eBook and Audiobook

CONVERSATION STARTERS

1. What did you know about Catherine the Great before reading this book? Were there things you learned from the book that matched your previous impressions of her? What did you learn about her that surprised you?

2. How important were Catherine's memoirs to the portrait Massie draws of her? What aspects of Catherine and her early life would we have missed had she not written her memoirs? What reasons might she have had for concluding them at the point she did and not writing about the years after 1758?

3. Johanna's early rejection stung Catherine, and her mother's domineering and difficult nature later caused Catherine pain and trouble. However, does Joanna deserve credit for having the ambition that led her daughter to an extraordinary life? How would you judge Johanna as a mother, both from a contemporary perspective and from the perspective of the eighteenth-century society in which she lived?

4. How did Catherine change from the docile girl who acted to please her husband in all things into the coup leader who marched to dethrone him? What were the most important steps in this evolution? Which qualities of the future Empress were already there in the Sophia who came to Russia, and which changed along the way?

5. Massie notes that "Zavadovsky—unique among her lovers—coveted neither honors nor riches." What role did Catherine's position and power play in her lovers' feelings for her? Which (if any) of these men would you say truly loved her?

6. Massie calls Potemkin "a lover and partner who gave her almost everything she wanted." Do you agree with this assessment? Which of Catherine's lovers do you think was most suited to her? Was there one with whom you could imagine her finding happiness in a long-lasting relationship, had the circumstances of her life been different?

7. "Voltaire began to see in her an enlightened monarch who might work to apply the principles of justice and tolerance he proclaimed." How much did Catherine work to do so? Would you call Catherine "an enlightened monarch"?

8. Are there strategies and tactics employed by Catherine, both in her acquisition of the throne and in her reign, that you see being used by leaders in politics and government today?

9. Overall, did you come away from the book finding Catherine an admirable leader? Why or why not?

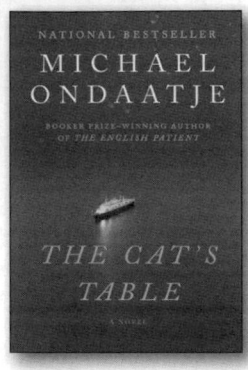

THE CAT'S TABLE
By Michael Ondaatje

In the early 1950s, an eleven-year-old boy in Colombo boards a ship bound for England. At mealtimes he is seated at the "cat's table"—as far from the Captain's Table as can be—with a ragtag group of "insignificant" adults and two other boys, Cassius and Ramadhin. As the ship crosses the Indian Ocean, the boys tumble from one adventure to another, bursting all over the place like freed mercury. But there are other diversions as well: they are first exposed to the magical worlds of jazz, women, and literature by their eccentric fellow travelers, and together they spy on a shackled prisoner, his crime and fate a galvanizing mystery that will haunt them forever. By turns poignant and electrifying, *The Cat's Table* is a spellbinding story about the magical, often forbidden, discoveries of childhood, and a lifelong journey that begins unexpectedly with a spectacular sea voyage.

"Mesmerizing. . . . As he did in his great novel, The English Patient, *Ondaatje conjures images that pull strangers into the vivid rooms of his imagination, their detail illumined by his words."* —**The New York Times Book Review**

"A gorgeous piece of writing. . . . Ondaatje has always been capable of conjuring up mesmerizing images to draw in a reader, but with The Cat's Table *he holds back just enough so the lyricism doesn't overwhelm the story."* —**The Christian Science Monitor**

ABOUT THE AUTHOR: **Michael Ondaatje** is the author of five previous novels, a memoir, a nonfiction book on film, and several books of poetry. *The English Patient* won the Booker Prize; *Anil's Ghost* won the *Irish Times* International Fiction Prize, the Giller Prize, and the Prix Médicis. Born in Sri Lanka, Michael Ondaatje now lives in Toronto.

June 2012 | Trade Paperback | Fiction | 288 pp | $15.00 | ISBN 9780307744418
Vintage | randomhouse.com
Also available as: eBook and Audiobook

CONVERSATION STARTERS

1. How is the voyage itself a metaphor for childhood?
2. Why do you think the opening passages of the book are told in third person?
3. We are 133 pages into the novel before Ondaatje gives us an idea of what year it is. How does he use time—or the sense of timelessness—to propel the story?
4. For several characters—the three boys and Emily among them—the journey represents a loss of innocence. For whom does it have the greatest impact?
5. Discuss the importance of some of the seemingly minor characters at the table: Mr. Mazappa, Mr. Fonseka, Mr. Nevil. What do they contribute to the story?
6. "What is interesting and important happens mostly in secret, in places where there is no power," the narrator realizes. "Nothing much of lasting value ever happens at the head table, held together by a familiar rhetoric. Those who already have power continue to glide along the familiar rut they have made for themselves." How does this prove true over the course of the novel?
7. How do the narrator's experiences breaking and entering with the Baron change his way of looking at the world?
8. The narrator refers to Ramadhin as "the saint of our clandestine family." What does he mean?
9. When describing the collapse of his marriage, the narrator says, "Massi said that sometimes, when things overwhelmed me, there was a trick or a habit I had: I turned myself into something that did not belong anywhere. I trusted nothing I was told, not even what I witnessed." What made him behave this way? How did it affect his marriage?
10. What was your reaction to the revelations about Miss Lasqueti?
11. How do you think her letter to Emily might have changed the events on board the *Oronsay*? Why didn't she send it?
12. Discuss Emily's relationship with Asuntha. Did she, as the narrator suggests, see herself in the deaf girl?
13. When Emily says to the narrator, "I don't think you can love me into safety," to what is she referring? What is the danger, decades after the voyage?
14. The narrator wishes to protect Emily, Cassius has Asuntha, and Ramadhin has Heather Cave. "What happened that the three of us had a desire to protect others seemingly less secure than ourselves?" How would you answer that question?

CONQUISTADORA

By Esmeralda Santiago

As a young girl growing up in Spain, Ana Larragoity Cubillas is powerfully drawn to Puerto Rico by the diaries of an ancestor who traveled there with Ponce de Leon. And in handsome twin brothers Ramón and Inocente—both in love with Ana—she finds a way to get there. Marrying Ramón at the young age of eighteen, she travels across the ocean to Hacienda los Gemelos, a remote sugar plantation the brothers have inherited on the island. But soon the Civil War erupts in the United States, and Ana finds her livelihood, and perhaps even her life, threatened by the very people on whose backs her wealth has been built: the hacienda's slaves, whose richly drawn stories unfold alongside her own in this epic novel of love, discovery, and adventure.

"Santiago's storytelling is thrilling. . . . Conquistadora *is a triumph."*
—*The Washington Post*

"Extraordinary. . . . . An outstanding story, full of pathos, tropical sensuality, and violence—but it also poses uncomfortable moral questions readers are forced to consider . . . Storytelling genius . . . Conquistadora *is a book-group must." —Booklist* (starred review)

About the Author: **Esmeralda Santiago** is the author of the memoirs *When I Was Puerto Rican, Almost a Woman* (which she adapted into a Peabody Award–winning film for PBS's Masterpiece Theatre) and *The Turkish Lover;* the novel *América's Dream;* and a children's book, *A Doll for Navidades.* Her work has appeared in *The New York Times, The Boston Globe,* and *House & Garden,* among other publications, and on NPR's *All Things Considered* and *Morning Edition.* Born in San Juan, Puerto Rico, she lives in New York.

July 2012 | Trade Paperback | Fiction | 432 pp | $15.95 | ISBN 9780307388599
Vintage 2012 | randomhouse.com | esmeraldasantiago.com
Also available as: eBook and Audiobook

CONVERSATION STARTERS

1. Santiago's epigraph is an excerpt from "Adam" by William Carlos Williams: "Underneath the whisperings/ of tropic nights/there is a darker whispering/that death invents especially/for northern men/whom the tropics/ have come to hold." Why do you think she chose this passage?
2. How familiar were you with the history Santiago provides in the opening section of the novel—*El Encuentro*/The Encounter: November 19, 1493?
3. As the book begins, how do you feel about Ana? Is she a likable character? What one word would you use to describe her?
4. How does Ana's attitude toward slavery, and her own slaves, change over the course of the novel? How does she change in general and why?
5. Discuss Ana's relationship with Elena. What draws these women together—and what drives them apart? How do their motivations for getting married differ?
6. Why do you think Ana agrees to sleep with both Ramón and Inocente? Does she have a choice in the matter?
7. Why does Los Gemelos become so important to Ana? Why won't she leave—and why would she be willing to go so far as to trade her son for the plantation? Did you understand her motivation for this?
8. Why does Ana refer to her slaves as "*nuestra gente*" ("our people")?
9. Why does Severo want Ana as his wife, although it is Consuelo who makes him happy? Do you think he can love these two women at once?
10. What is the significance of the house Severo builds for Ana? Why does he name it El Destino?
11. As the novel ends, the American Civil War has already begun to change life in Puerto Rico—perhaps especially for the hacienda's slaves, who are inspired by "*el libertador* Abrámlincon." How is the history of slavery in Puerto Rico similar to, or different from, the history of slavery in America? What surprised you most about Santiago's depiction of the slaves' daily lives?
12. How does *Conquistadora* compare to other postcolonial literature you've read—stories that take place in Africa, Asia, and the Americas?
13. Does Ana earn the designation *conquistadora*? If she were alive today, what do you think she would do for a living?
14. What do you think lies ahead for Ana and Severo? What about Segundo, who will inherit their land and the hacienda? And the slaves at the hacienda?

THE CONVERT
A Tale of Exile and Extremism

By Deborah Baker

* A 2011 National Book Award Finalist *

* A *Publishers Weekly* Best Book of the Year *

What drives a young woman raised in a postwar New York City suburb to convert to Islam, abandon her country and faith, and embrace a life of exile in Pakistan? *The Convert* tells the story of how Margaret Marcus of Larchmont became Maryam Jameelah of Lahore, one of the most trenchant and celebrated voices of Islam's argument with the West. A cache of Maryam's letters to her parents in the archives of the New York Public Library sends acclaimed biographer Deborah Baker on her own odyssey into the labyrinthine heart of twentieth-century Islam. As she assembles the pieces of a singularly perplexing life, Baker finds herself captive to questions raised by Maryam's journey. Is her story just another bleak chapter in a so-called clash of civilizations? Or does it signify something else entirely? And is the life depicted in Maryam's letters home and in her books an honest reflection of the one she lived?

"Sexual secrets? Suspense? Drama? Reversals? They're all here. . . . [Deborah] Baker's captivating account conveys the instability, faith, politics, and improbable cultural migration that make Jameelah's life story so difficult to sum up yet impossible to dismiss." —**The New York Times Book Review**

"Spellbinding." —**Library Journal**, starred review

"[A] stellar biography that doubles as a mediation on the fraught relationship between America and the Muslim world." —**Publishers Weekly,** starred review

ABOUT THE AUTHOR: **Deborah Baker** is the author of *In Extremis: The Life of Laura Riding*, a finalist for a Pulitzer Prize, as well as *A Blue Hand: The Beats in India*. She divides her time between Calcutta, Goa, and Brooklyn.

September 2012 | Trade Paperback | Nonfiction | 272 pp | $15.00 | ISBN 978155597627९
Graywolf Press | graywolfpress.org | deborahbaker.net
Also available as: eBook and Audiobook

CONVERSATION STARTERS

1. Did you find Maryam Jameelah to be a sympathetic or admirable figure? Why or why not? Were there any parts of Jameelah's tale that you found you could personally relate to?

2. What do you think drew Deborah Baker to Jameelah as a biographical subject? Despite their very different lives, do you think Baker and Jameelah share any value systems or life experiences that make them particularly well matched as biographer and subject? Why do you think Baker chose to bring her own voice and point of view into the narrative of Jameelah's story? How does this differ from other biographical or nonfiction works you've read?

3. Baker points out how mental illness was treated and viewed in the 1950s and 1960s. How do you think Jameelah's life might have unfolded differently if she were a teenager today? How did the revelation of her illness impact your reading of her letters?

4. Did you find any conflict between the relative freedoms Jameelah enjoyed as a religious leader and renowned ideologue and the more traditional roles assigned to women via the teachings of Mawlana Mawdudi?

5. Most of Jameelah's letters in *The Convert* are addressed to her parents. Why do you think she continued to maintain this connection, which seemed so vital to her existence, despite having renounced her parents' country, culture, and religious beliefs?

6. Baker conducted the majority of her research for *The Convert* at the New York Public Library, where Jameelah's letters are archived. Why do you think Jameelah chose to not only make her letters available to the public, but to entrust them to a Western institution? Why not send her archives to an institution in Pakistan?

7. At the end of *The Convert*, Baker writes, "In her most recent letter to me, Maryam asked that I send her two copies of a *National Geographic* book of photographs. I'm still trying to decide what books I will send." What books would you send to Maryam Jameelah, and why?

8. What do you think motivated Mawlana Mawdudi to take Jameelah into his home?

9. What do you think Jameelah would make of *The Convert*? Do you think she would find it to be a fair portrait? Does it matter?

THE DARK MONK
A Hangman's Daughter Tale

By Oliver Pötzsch

The anticipated followup to the international bestseller, *The Hangman's Daughter*.

1660: Winter has settled thick over a sleepy village in the Bavarian Alps, ensuring every farmer and servant is indoors the night a parish priest discovers he's been poisoned. As numbness creeps up his body, he summons the last of his strength to scratch a cryptic sign in the frost.

Following a trail of riddles, hangman Jakob Kuisl; his headstrong daughter Magdalena; and the town physician's son team up with the priest's aristocratic sister to investigate. What they uncover will lead them back to the Crusades, unlocking a troubled history of internal church politics and sending them on a chase for a treasure of the Knights Templar.

But they're not the only ones after the legendary fortune. A team of dangerous and mysterious monks is always close behind, tracking their every move, speaking Latin in the shadows, giving off a strange, intoxicating scent. And to throw the hangman off their trail, they have ensured he is tasked with capturing a band of thieves roving the countryside attacking solitary travelers and spreading panic.

"Pötzsch does an excellent job of plunking the reader down in seventeenth-century Germany. . . . Readers will also appreciate the nice balance between drama, suspense, and humor: this is a serious story, Pötzsch seems to be saying, but it's OK to have some fun with it. At least two more books in the series are forthcoming, and they will be most welcome." —Booklist

ABOUT THE AUTHOR: **Oliver Pötzsch**, born in 1970, has worked for years as a scriptwriter for Bavarian television. He is a descendant of one of Bavaria's leading dynasties of executioners. Pötzsch lives in Munich with his family.

June 2012 | Trade Paperback | Fiction | 512 pp | $18.00 | ISBN 9780547807683
Houghton Mifflin Harcourt | hmhbooks.com
Also available as: eBook

CONVERSATION STARTERS

1. There are a number of allusions to the Templar text Ordinis Templorum Historia and Latin quotes throughout the novel. Explain these references: How do they help to solve the mystery?
2. Explain the various roles religion plays in *The Dark Monk*.
3. Augustin Bonenmayr is seeking the True Cross of Christ—"It will adorn this church, and crowds of pilgrims will once again come flocking to Steingaden!"—and is willing to do anything to obtain it, even kill. How does history show that religious fervor always leads to violence?
4. The novel opens with a quote from Aristotle, Poetics, XXIV: "We delight in marvelous things. One proof of that is that everyone embellishes somewhat when telling a story in the assumption he is pleasing his listener." How is this sentiment explored in *The Dark Monk*? Who in the novel embellishes their story? What, if any, punishment is given to this person?
5. Compare how Oliver Pötzsch fleshes out the male and female characters. Do you think he does a better job with one gender? Why do you think he chose Magdalena Kuisl instead of Jakob Kuisl to title the series after?
6. Discuss the significance of Andreas Koppmeyer. What is his role in the story?
7. How does Benedikta serve as a foil to Magdalena? Who, if anyone, fills that role for Simon?
8. Why is Simon "both attracted and repelled" by Benedikta?
9. How does Simon's superficial love of fashion and appearance blind him to potential danger?
10. How much, if any, has Johann Lechner changed since the first novel? Is Lechner still willing to do whatever it takes to ensure the safety of Schongau?
11. Explain Kuisl's worry for Simon while having hardly any for his daughter, Magdalena, while she is in Augsburg. Was it was a wise decision to send Magdalena, a young woman, to Augsburg without an escort?
12. What do you make of Jakob Kuisl's distinction "I'm a hangman, but not a murderer"?
13. What are some of the pleasures and drawbacks of reading historical novels, especially those with a grounding in reality?

DARK PLACES

By Gillian Flynn

Libby Day was seven when her mother and two sisters were murdered in "The Satan Sacrifice of Kinnakee, Kansas." As her family lay dying, little Libby fled their tiny farmhouse into the freezing January snow. She lost some fingers and toes, but she survived—and famously testified that her fifteen-year-old brother, Ben, was the killer. Twenty-five years later, Ben sits in prison, and troubled Libby lives off the dregs of a trust created by well-wishers who've long forgotten her.

The Kill Club is a macabre secret society obsessed with notorious crimes. When they locate Libby and pump her for details—proof they hope may free Ben—Libby hatches a plan to profit off her tragic history. For a fee, she'll reconnect with the players from that night and report her findings to the club . . . And maybe she'll admit her testimony wasn't so solid after all.

As Libby's search takes her from shabby Missouri strip clubs to abandoned Oklahoma tourist towns, the narrative flashes back to January 2, 1985. The events of that day are relayed through the eyes of Libby's doomed family members—including Ben, a loner whose rage over his shiftless father and their failing farm have driven him into a disturbing friendship with the new girl in town. Piece by piece, the unimaginable truth emerges, and Libby finds herself right back where she started—on the run from a killer.

"Flynn's well-paced story deftly shows the fallibility of memory and the lies a child tells herself to get through a trauma." —The New Yorker

ABOUT THE AUTHOR: **Gillian Flynn** is the author of *The New York Times* bestseller *Dark Places*, which was a *The New Yorker* Reviewers' Favorite, *Weekend* TODAY Top Summer Read, *Publishers Weekly* Best Book of 2009, and *Chicago Tribune* Favorite Fiction choice; and the Dagger Award winner *Sharp Objects*, which was an Edgar nominee for Best First novel, a BookSense pick, and a Barnes & Noble Discover selection. Her work has been published in twenty-eight countries. She lives in Chicago with her husband and son.

May 2010 | Trade Paperback | Fiction | 368 pp | $14.00 | ISBN 9780307341570
Broadway | randomhouse.com | gillian-flynn.com
Also available as: eBook and Audiobook
Gillian Flynn's other **Reading Group Choices'** selections: *Gone Girl* and *Sharp Objects*

CONVERSATION STARTERS

1. Did you like Libby as a character? Do you think the author intended for her to be likeable?
2. Why has Libby ignored Jim Jeffreys's advice to earn an income for so many years? Do you believe she feels she's earned the money she's been gifted by strangers? What is her attitude toward money?
3. Like others Libby meets during her investigation, Barb Eichel seems pleased to have been contacted, having "wondered if you'd ever get in touch." Why did Barb wait for Libby to come to her? Did Barb do enough to remedy the harm she thinks her book has done?
4. In considering the case of the missing girl Lisette Stephens, Libby thinks to herself, "There was nothing to solve . . . She just vanished for no reason anyone could think of, except she was pretty." Do you think it's strange that Libby considers this an uninteresting case? What does her attitude toward Lisette say about her view of her own family's murder? Was there something to "solve" in the Days' murder?
5. One of the appealing aspects of the Day case (according to Lyle) is the role of children as instigators, victims, and unreliable witnesses. Do you see any similarities among Krissi's accusation, Libby's false eyewitness account, and Lyle's role in the California fires? Were these children to blame for their mistakes? In what ways did they attempt to right the wrongs they caused?
6. "No one ever forgives me for anything," one character says. What role does forgiveness play in Dark Places? Which characters should be more forgiving? Less?
7. Patty Day frequently worries whether she is a good mother. What do you think? How does the book depict parents in general? Whom do you consider the "good" and "bad" parents in the book?
8. Did you think Ben was guilty? Does the author intend for us to doubt him?
9. Why doesn't Diane return Libby's phone calls? What does she mean at the end of the book when she says, "I knew you could do it . . . I knew you could . . . try just a little harder"? Do you like Diane?
10. Do you think Ben will find Crystal? What do you imagine their reunion would be like?
11. Libby is a liar, a manipulator, a kleptomaniac, and an opportunist. Does she have any redeeming qualities? Are you able to empathize with her? If so, why?

DEATH COMES TO PEMBERLEY

By P. D. James

It is 1803, six years since Elizabeth and Darcy embarked on their life together at Pemberley, Darcy's magnificent estate. Their peaceful, orderly world seems almost unassailable. Elizabeth has found her footing as the chatelaine of the great house. They have two fine sons, Fitzwilliam and Charles. Elizabeth's sister Jane and her husband, Bingley, live nearby; her father visits often; there is optimistic talk about the prospects of marriage for Darcy's sister Georgiana. And preparations are under way for their much-anticipated annual autumn ball.

Then, on the eve of the ball, the patrician idyll is shattered. A coach careens up the drive carrying Lydia, Elizabeth's disgraced sister, who with her husband, the very dubious Wickham, has been banned from Pemberley. She stumbles out of the carriage, hysterical, shrieking that Wickham has been murdered. With shocking suddenness, Pemberley is plunged into a frightening mystery.

"A sparkling curio that will appeal to both Janeites and Jamesites." —Daily Telegraph

"Jane Austen herself would have applauded." —The Spectator

ABOUT THE AUTHOR: **P. D. James** is the author of twenty previous books, most of which have been filmed and broadcast on television in the United States and other countries. She spent thirty years in various departments of the British Civil Service, including the Police and Criminal Law Departments of Great Britain's Home Office. She has served as a magistrate and as a governor of the BBC. In 2000 she celebrated her eightieth birthday and published her autobiography, *Time to Be in Earnest*. The recipient of many prizes and honors, she was created Baroness James of Holland Park in 1991 and was inducted into the International Crime Writing Hall of Fame in 2008. She lives in London and Oxford.

January 2013 | Trade Paperback* | Fiction | 320 pp | $15.00 | ISBN 9780307950659
Vintage | randomhouse.com | paulpjjames.com/book/
Also availabe as : eBook and Audiobook
*Hardcover jacket pictured above.

....

CONVERSATION STARTERS

1. What do you notice about the prose style James adopts for this novel? What relationship does it bear to the style of Jane Austen?

2. James has provided many links in the introductory chapters that provide both the backstory of and continuity with *Pride and Prejudice*. How successful is the bridge that she creates?

3. What do you think of James's re-creation of Austen's characters, particularly Elizabeth and Darcy? How are they changed, and how are they similar to the originals?

4. The extensive woodland on Darcy's estate, with its "torn and hanging twigs," its "tangled bushes," and its confusion, presents a strong contrast to the order and rationality of the household and the cultivated grounds. What might P. D. James be suggesting about Elizabeth and Darcy's world by giving the woodland such a strong presence in the novel?

5. How do you judge the character of Wickham, given the further development provided by P. D. James? Is he sympathetic? Is he careless and narcissistic? Do you agree with the Reverend Cornbinder that he is capable of remaking himself in America?

6. Wickham is about to be condemned to death when two surprising things happen: Mrs. Younge rushes from the courtroom and is crushed under the wheels of a coach, and a letter of confession arrives from William Bidwell. What do you think of these sudden plot twists?

7. Darcy is deeply affected by the murder on his estate. Why does it shake his sense of identity and his earldom? How does the story Wickham tells about his romance with Louisa, and the motivations surrounding it, make the troubled relationship between Darcy and Wickham more clear? Why is Lydia entirely absent from the story that Wickham tells?

8. What do you think of Louisa's resolution to marry Joseph Billings and live at Highmarten, as well as the adoption of baby Georgie by Mrs. Martin? Does this seem like a good outcome for them?

9. James has some fun including references to other Jane Austen novels. Did you identify the references to *Emma* and *Persuasion*?

10. P. D. James has invented a satisfying new episode in the life of Elizabeth's troublesome sister Lydia and her ill-chosen husband. What further episodes would you and your group members come up with, if you were to write a sequel to *Pride and Prejudice*?

A DIFFERENT KIND OF NORMAL
Cathy Lamb

Jaden Bruxelle knows that life is precious. She sees it in her work as a hospice nurse, a job filled with compassion and humor even on the saddest days. And she sees it in Tate, the boy she has raised as her son ever since her sister gave him up at birth. Tate is seventeen, academically brilliant, funny, and loving. He's also a talented basketball player despite having been born with an abnormally large head—something Jaden's mother blames on a family curse. Jaden dismisses that as nonsense, just as she ignores the legends about witches and magic in the family.

Over the years, Jaden has focused all her energy on her job and on sheltering Tate from the world. Tate, for his part, just wants to be a regular kid. Through his blog, he's slowly reaching out, finding his voice. He wants to try out for the Varsity basketball team. He wants his mom to focus on her own life for a change, maybe even date again.

Jaden knows she needs to let go—of Tate, of her fears and anger, and of the responsibilities she uses as a shield. And through a series of unexpected events and revelations, she's about to learn how. Because as dear as life may be, its only real value comes when we are willing to live it fully, even if that means risking it all.

"Will definitely warm the hearts of readers, especially given that the protagonist's deformed, yet positive, young teen has the ability to make the most of his imperfections." —RT Book Reviews

ABOUT THE AUTHOR: **Cathy Lamb**, the author of *Julia's Chocolates*, *The Last Time I Was Me*, and *Henry's Sisters*, lives in Oregon. She is married with three children. She writes late at night when it's just her and the moon and a few shooting stars.

August 2012 | Trade Paperback | Fiction | 416 pp | $15.00 | ISBN 9780758259394
Kensington Books | kensingtonbooks.com | cathylamb.net
Also available as: eBook

CONVERSATION STARTERS

1. Who was your favorite character? Why? If you could spend the day with one character, who would it be, and what would you do?

2. Jaden said, "Another reason I became a hospice nurse was because I crave raw, honest relationships and have zero patience for superficiality. When you are working with people who are dying, all pretenses are off. There is no shallowness, no silliness. I don't have the patience for relationships that float and skim across the top of human existence, relationships that have no depth or that are based on shopping, manicures, gossip, men, clubbing, etc. I want real relationships." Can you relate to this? Was Jaden a competent hospice nurse? Did it make sense for her to move on to another career by the end of the book?

3. What was your favorite scene in the book and why?

4. Was Jaden right, as a mother, to allow Tate to play basketball? What would you have done?

5. Brooke said, "I destroyed a lot of lives to make money. I am up nights wondering how many people I killed who took the drugs I sold them. I am up nights wondering how many pregnant women took my drugs and what that did to their babies. I am up nights wondering how many mothers' sons are now addicted to my drugs, how many fathers' daughters are drugged out and doing scary things with terrible men because they're addicts, like I did." Do you like Brooke? Was her drug addiction portrayed correctly? Do you think she will stay clean? Why or why not?

6. What are the themes of *A Different Kind of Normal*?

7. What did the seasons symbolize? What did the greenhouse symbolize? The herbs and spices? The Canterbury bells, hollyhocks, lilies, irises, sweet peas, cosmos, red poppies, peonies, and rows of roses, which all the women in the family grew?

8. Jaden says, "I'm Earth Momma with an explosive temper meets cowgirl. She's [Rowan] firecracker meets perfume." How was Rowan as a parent? A grandparent? Using the same type of phraseology, how would you describe yourself?

9. How have the stories of Faith and Grace impacted Jaden's life? Why did the author include the family history, complete with spells, witches, and a velvet satchel? How did it work for you as a reader?

A DISCOVERY OF WITCHES

By Deborah E. Harkness

In a sparkling debut, *A Discovery of Witches* became the "it" book of early 2011, bringing Deborah Harkness into the spotlight and galvanizing fans around the world. In this tale of passion and obsession, Diana Bishop, a young scholar and the descendant of witches, discovers a long-lost and enchanted alchemical manuscript deep in Oxford's Bodleian Library. Its reappearance summons a fantastical underworld, which she navigates with her leading man, vampire geneticist Matthew Clairmont. Harkness has created a universe to rival those of Anne Rice, Diana Gabaldon, and Elizabeth Kostova, and she adds a scholar's depth to this riveting story of magic and suspense. And the story continues in Book Two, *Shadow of Night*.

"An inventive addition to the supernatural craze. . . . Historian Harkness's racy paranormal romance has exciting amounts of spells, kisses and battles, and is recounted with enchanting, page-turning panache." —**Marie Claire**

"A wonderfully imaginative grown-up fantasy with all the magic of Harry Potter *and* Twilight." —**People**

"Intelligent and off-the-wall, it will be irresistible to Twilight *fans."* —**The Sunday Times**

ABOUT THE AUTHOR: **Deborah E. Harkness** is a scholar and writer specializing in the history of science and medicine. She has received numerous awards, including Fulbright, Guggenheim, and National Humanities Center fellowships. Currently a professor of history at the University of Southern California, her most recent academic publication is *The Jewel House: Elizabethan London and the Scientific Revolution*. This is her first novel.

December 2011 | Trade Paperback | Fiction | 592 pp | $16.00 | ISBN 9780143119685
Penguin Books | us.penguingroup.com | deborahharkness.com
Also available as: eBook and Audiobook

CONVERSATION STARTERS

1. Diana's mother says that fear is "the strongest force on earth." What does she mean? Do you agree?

2. Early in the novel, Harkness describes the typical personalities and physical traits of daemons, witches, and vampires. If you could be any one of these beings, which would you choose and why?

3. Who is the Congregation? Is it a force for good or a force for evil?

4. What happened to Diana's parents? What were they trying to hide?

5. Diana studies alchemy, which she defines as a type of "science with magic" used to explore and understand unexplained phenomena. Do you use astrology, fortune-telling, or ESP to provide a deeper understanding of events in your own life?

6. Why is Diana and Matthew's love forbidden? Have you ever loved someone whom your family or friends thought was inappropriate? How did their reaction influence your feelings?

7. Most of the book is told from Diana's perspective, yet a few chapters are written in the third person. Why? What feature or purpose unites those chapters?

8. Diana and Matthew travel back to the sixteenth century. If you had the power to time walk, as she does, what period in history would you visit?

9. In chapter 31, Diana remembers the bedtime story her mother told her as a child. In what ways does that story foreshadow the events of Diana's life?

10. Harkness presents the use of witchcraft not only as an otherworldly ability but also as a part of everyday life; for example, Diana uses a spell to fix her washing machine. Which example of the novel's blending of the magical with the mundane did you find most entertaining or creative? If you could use magic in your daily life, what would you use it for?

11. Look at the last page of the book. What is the significance of the blood and mercury? What is the reason behind the sense of relief felt in the house? What does the last sentence of the book mean?

THE DOVEKEEPERS
By Alice Hoffman

Nearly two thousand years ago, nine hundred Jews held out for months against armies of Romans on Masada, a mountain in the Judean desert. According to the ancient historian Josephus, two women and five children survived.

Based on this tragic and iconic event, Hoffman's novel is a spellbinding tale of four extraordinarily bold, resourceful, and sensuous women, each of whom has come to Masada by a different path. Yael's mother died in childbirth, and her father, an expert assassin, never forgave her for that death. Revka, a village baker's wife, watched the murder of her daughter by Roman soldiers; she brings to Masada her young grandsons, rendered mute by what they have witnessed. Aziza is a warrior's daughter, raised as a boy, a fearless rider and expert marksman who finds passion with a fellow soldier. Shirah, born in Alexandria, is wise in the ways of ancient magic and medicine, a woman with uncanny insight and power. The lives of these four complex and fiercely independent women intersect in the desperate days of the siege. All are dovekeepers, and all are also keeping secrets.

"Spellbinding . . . Ancient times come to shimmering life in this superb novel."
—Parade

ABOUT THE AUTHOR: **Alice Hoffman** was born in New York City in 1952 and grew up on Long Island. Hoffman's first novel, *Property Of*, was written at the age of twenty-one. She has published a total of twenty-eight works of fiction. Her novel, *Here on Earth*, was an Oprah Book Club choice. *Practical Magic* was made into a Warner film starring Sandra Bullock and Nicole Kidman. Hoffman's work has been published in more than twenty translations and more than one hundred foreign editions. Hoffman is currently a visiting research scholar at the Women's Studies Research Center at Brandeis University. She lives in Boston.

April 2012 | Trade Paperback | Fiction | 528 pp | $16.00 | ISBN 9781451617481
Scribner | simonandschuster.com | alicehoffman.com
Also available as: eBook and Audiobook

CONVERSATION STARTERS

1. The novel is split into four principal parts, with each of the main characters narrating one section. Which of these women did you find most appealing, and why?
2. Yael describes her relationship with Ben Simon as "a destroying sort of love." What does she mean by that? Are there other relationships in the novel that could be described in the same way?
3. The figure of Wynn, "The Man from the North," who comes to serve the women in the dovecote, is based upon archeological finds at Masada. In what ways does Wynn come to bring the women together? How would you compare Yael's relationship with Ben Simon to her relationship with Wynn?
4. How do Shirah's daughters react to the intimate friendship that develops between Yael and their mother? Is Shirah a good mother or not?
5. What do you make of Channa's attempt, essentially, to kidnap Yael's baby Arieh? Is Channa different from the other major female characters in the book? Do you find your opinion of her changes?
6. "You don't fight for peace, sister," Nahara tells Aziza. "You embrace it." What do you think of Nahara's decision to join the Essenes? Is she naïve or a true believer? Do you see similarities between the Essenes and the early Christian movement?
7. Revka's son-in-law, the warrior known as The Man from the Valley, asks Aziza, "Did you not think this is what the world was like?" How would you describe the circumstances of this question? After all her training for battle, why is Aziza unprepared for the experience of attacking a village filled with women and children?
8. In the final pages of the book, Yael sums up those who perished at Masada, remembering them as "men who refused to surrender and women who were ruled by devotion." Do you agree with this?
9. For the women at Masada, dreams contain important messages, ghosts meddle in the lives of the living, and spells can remedy a number of human ills. How does their culture's acceptance of the mystical compare to our culture's view on such things today? How do they compare to your own views?
10. Women's knowledge in *The Dovekeepers* is handed down from mother to daughter, sister to sister, friend to friend. Do you see any connection with the way in which your own family stories are handed down through the generations?

THE EXPATS
By Chris Pavone

Kate Moore is a working mother, struggling to make ends meet, to raise children, to keep a spark in her marriage . . . and to maintain an increasingly unbearable life-defining secret. So when her husband is offered a lucrative job in Luxembourg, she jumps at the chance to leave behind her double-life, to start anew.

She begins to reinvent herself as an expat, finding her way in a language she doesn't speak, doing the housewifely things she's never before done—playdates and coffee mornings, daily cooking and never-ending laundry. Meanwhile, her husband works incessantly, at a job Kate has never understood, for a banking client she's not allowed to know. He's becoming distant and evasive; she's getting lonely and bored.

Then another American couple arrives. Kate soon becomes suspicious that these people are not who they say they are, and she's terrified that her own past is catching up to her. So Kate begins to dig, to peel back the layers of deception that surround her. She discovers fake offices and shell corporations and a hidden gun, a mysterious farmhouse and numbered accounts with bewildering sums of money, and finally unravels the mind-boggling long-play con that threatens her family, her marriage, and her life.

"Sly. . . . Pavone strengthens this book with a string of head-spinning revelations in its last pages. . . . The tireless scheming of all four principals truly exceeds all sane expectations." —The New York Times

ABOUT THE AUTHOR: **Chris Pavone** grew up in Brooklyn and graduated from Cornell. For nearly two decades he was a book editor and ghostwriter; he is also the author of The Wine Log. Chris and his family have lived in Luxembourg, but recently returned to New York City. The Expats is his first novel.

March 2012 | Hardcover | Fiction | 336 pp | $26.00 | ISBN 9780307956354
Paperback available January 2013 (ISBN 9780770435721; $15.00)
Crown | randomhouse.com | chrispavone.com
Also available as: eBook and Audiobook
To inquire about having the author visit your reading group via phone or video chat, please email crownreadinggroups@randomhouse.com

CONVERSATION STARTERS

1. How does Kate's sense of self shift throughout the novel? In the end, how does she reconcile the roles of wife, mom, and adrenaline-seeking agent?

2. After working hard to keep her own career a secret from Dexter, why is it hard for Kate to accept his secrecy about his job? Was she setting a double standard or just responding to her well-honed instincts?

3. What were your initial theories about Julia and Bill, and the "Today" scenes?

4. Kate was well suited to her job when she led a solitary life. What did the CIA give her in lieu of love? As she realizes that Dexter and her family are all she has, how does her understanding of love change?

5. What is Hayden's role in Kate's life? Do you have a Hayden to rely on?

6. How do Kate and Dexter feel about the power of breadwinners in a marriage? What does their story say about resenting a spouse who doesn't seem to be contributing (Dexter in America) versus resenting a spouse who seems to be a workaholic (Dexter in Luxembourg)? In the end, which of the novel's characters prove to be the most materialistic?

7. Kate is haunted by the Torres episode. How did this continue to define her decision making and actions years later? If you were ever in a situation like this, how far would you go to protect your family?

8. Dexter often cites human gullibility as a weakness in I.T. security. Discuss the characters who let their guard down for love, vanity, sex, wealth, or other lures. What ultimately makes Dexter gullible? Does his gullibility make him blameless?

9. As the plot began to unfold, which revelations surprised you the most? What truth was buried beneath the layers of deception?

10. *The Expats* delivers a highly realistic portrayal of female agents, motherhood, and strong women who outsmart men. What is the effect of knowing that the book was written by a man?

11. Does it matter that the Colonel was bloodthirsty? Do the ends justify the means?

12. What does the novel say about trust and how it is earned? What do Kate and Dexter discover about the strength of their trust for each other?

FALLING TOGETHER

By Marisa de los Santos

Pen, Cat, and Will met on their first day of college and formed what seemed like a magical and lifelong bond, only to see their friendship break apart amid the realities of adulthood. When, after years of silence, Cat—the bewitching, charismatic center of their group—e-mails Pen and Will with an urgent request to meet at their college reunion, they can't refuse. But instead of a happy reconciliation, what awaits is a collision of past and present that sends Pen and Will, with Pen's five-year-old daughter and Cat's hostile husband in tow, on a journey across the world.

With her trademark wit, vivid prose, and gift for creating authentic, captivating characters, Marisa de los Santos returns with an emotionally resonant novel about our deepest human connections. As Pen and Will struggle to uncover the truth about Cat, they find more than they bargained for: startling truths about who they were before and who they are now. They must confront the reasons their friendship fell apart and discover how—and if—it can ever fall back together.

*"The mix of perfectly realized personalities and genuine emotion make this a winner." —**Publishers Weekly***

*"A satisfying novel about friends rediscovering one another—and confronting unwelcome truths—at their college reunion." —**People***

ABOUT THE AUTHOR: An award-winning poet and bestselling author with a Ph.D. in literature and creative writing, **Marisa de los Santos** lives in Wilmington, Delaware, with her husband, the children's book author David Teague, and their son and daughter. She's the author of the bestsellers *Love Walked In* and *Belong to Me*.

October 2012 | Trade Paperback | Fiction | 384 pp | $14.99 | ISBN 9780061670886
William Morrow Paperbacks | harpercollins.com
Also available as: eBook and Audiobook

CONVERSATION STARTERS

1. Describe Pen, Will, and Cat. What were they like as students and how has time changed who they are? All three of them have serious issues involving their fathers. Talk about how their relationships shaped their lives and their outlooks. How did each cope with their emotional wounds?

2. What makes friendships work between people? Why is it often difficult to sustain friendships as we get older? How can we sustain them? Is it sometimes better to let a friendship die? Have you ever enjoyed a friendship as special as that of the trio in the book? How did it impact your life? Can a person live without close friends?

3. Why do Pen and Will decide to go to the reunion after they receive Cat's email? What are they hoping for in attending? Can we turn back time and reunite in a fulfilling way or are the people we are today just too far removed from our past selves

4. When they meet at the reunion, Pen suggests they sum up the missing years in four sentences. Think about an old friend you haven't been in contact with for a while. Try it with members of your reading group. Think about what has happened since your last meeting and express it in a few sentences.

5. Pen has some interesting notions about love. She sees it as an "imperative." How does this view color how she sees love in her own life and in the lives of those around her—Will, Cat, Jason, Patrick, her mom? Would you say she's afraid of love?

6. Marisa de los Santos uses the image of falling in several ways throughout the novel. "There were people who could live on their own and be happy, and then there were people like Pen and Margaret who needed the falling together, the daily work of giving and taking and talk and touch." Discuss this example of falling and identify others.

7. While looking for Cat, Pen has her "jack-fish epiphany." Explain what insights she gleans, or as her colleague, Amelie describes it, "All is One and All is Different." Have you ever had a similar kind of "knowing moment" and when did it happen?

8. What finally gives Pen and Will the courage to share their feelings? Why does it take so long? Do you think they will stay in touch with Jason? Will Pen and Will last?

THE FLIGHT OF GEMMA HARDY
By Margot Livesey

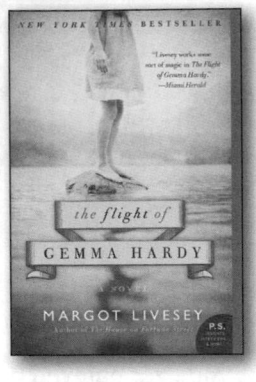

A captivating tale, set in Scotland in the early 1960s, that is both an homage to and a modern variation on the enduring classic *Jane Eyre*.

Fate has not been kind to Gemma Hardy. Orphaned by the age of ten, neglected by a bitter and cruel aunt, sent to a boarding school where she is both servant and student, young Gemma seems destined for a life of hardship and loneliness. Yet her bright spirit burns strong. Fiercely intelligent, singularly determined, Gemma overcomes each challenge and setback, growing stronger and more certain of her path. Now an independent young woman with dreams of the future, she accepts a position as an au pair on the remote and beautiful Orkney Islands.

But Gemma's biggest trial is about to begin . . . a journey of passion and betrayal, secrets and lies, redemption and discovery, that will lead her to a life she's never dreamed of.

"A delight . . . Livesey is a lovely, fluid writer" —**Sarah Towers, *The New York Times Book Review***

"Absorbing. . . . Ms. Livesey writes lovely, understated prose . . . [her] treks through the novel's pleasing natural landscapes . . . are almost as engaging as her navigation of Gemma's restless psyche." —**Sam Sacks, *Wall Street Journal***

ABOUT THE AUTHOR: **Margot Livesey** is the acclaimed author of the novels *The House on Fortune Street, Banishing Verona, Eva Moves the Furniture, The Missing World, Criminals,* and *Homework.* Her work has appeared in *The New Yorker, Vogue,* and *The Atlantic,* and she is the recipient of grants from both the National Endowment for the Arts and the Guggenheim Foundation. *The House on Fortune Street* won the 2009 L. L. Winship/PEN New England Award. Livesey was born in Scotland and grew up on the edge of the Highlands. She lives in the Boston area and is a Distinguished Writer-in-Residence at Emerson College.

June 2012 | Trade Paperback | Fiction | 480 pp | $15.99 | ISBN 9780062064233
Harper Perennial | harpercollins.com | margotlivesey.com
Also available as: eBook and large print

CONVERSATION STARTERS

1. Did Gemma's name take on new meanings for you in the course of reading the novel? What about the other names she uses at various points?

2. In the opening chapters, Gemma's aunt is quite hard-hearted, even cruel. Did your opinion of her change by the time you finished the novel?

3. How do you think the various landscapes that Gemma passes through help to change, or inform, her journey?

4. Gemma's uncle is a devout Christian. Do you think Gemma minds losing her faith? Do her childhood values continue to govern her actions as she matures into adulthood?

5. Throughout the novel there are various supernatural occurrences. What is their significance to the story and how do they impact Gemma?

6. How do Gemma's relationships with the various orphans she cares for deepen your understanding of her?

7. Gemma is at the mercy of chance but she also takes charge of her life and makes certain crucial decisions. How do you feel about those decisions?

8. What role do animals and birds play in Gemma's life?

9. If you've read Charlotte Bronte's *Jane Eyre*, are there places in *The Flight of Gemma Hardy* where you find yourself remembering Jane particularly vividly? How do those memories impact your reading of *Gemma*?

10. Did *The Flight of Gemma Hardy* make you think of other orphan stories beyond *Jane Eyre*? Why are orphan stories so endlessly appealing?

THE FORGOTTEN AFFAIRS OF YOUTH

By Alexander McCall Smith

Isabel and her fiancé know who they are and where they come from. But not everybody is so fortunate. Jane Cooper, a visiting Australian philosopher on sabbatical in Edinburgh, has more questions than answers. Adopted at birth, Jane is trying to find her biological father, but all she knows about him is that he was a student in Edinburgh years ago. When she asks for Isabel's help in this seemingly impossible search . . . well, of course Isabel obliges.

But Isabel also manages to find time for her own concerns: her young son, Charlie, already walking and talking; her housekeeper, Grace, whose spiritualist has lately been doubling as a financial advisor; her niece Cat's latest relationship; and the pressing question of when and how Isabel and Jamie should finally get married.

Should the forgotten affairs of youth be left in the past, or can the memories help us understand the present?

"You needn't be a series-long admirer of Isabel Dalhousie to be beguiled by this curious philosopher and casual sleuth . . . Isabel believes only the examined life is worth living, and fearlessly so . . . It makes [her] a heroine worth following, even through this quiet, more reflective foray."
—Publishers Weekly

About the Author: **Alexander McCall Smith** is the author of the beloved bestselling *No. 1 Ladies' Detective Agency* series, the *Isabel Dalhousie* series, the *Portuguese Irregular Verbs* series, the *44 Scotland Street* series, and the *Corduroy Mansions* series. He is also the author of numerous children's books. He is professor emeritus of medical law at the University of Edinburgh and has served with many national and international organizations concerned with bioethics. He was born in what is now known as Zimbabwe and taught law at the University of Botswana. He lives in Scotland.

October 2012 | Trade Paperback* | Fiction | 288 pp | $14.95 | ISBN 9780307739407
Anchor | randomhouse.com | mccallsmith.com
Also available as: eBook
*Hardcover jacket pictured above.

CONVERSATION STARTERS

1. Isabel and Jane have an immediate rapport: "Their conversation had started in the deep end, unlike most conversations, which launched themselves into the shallowest of shallows." Do you agree with Isabel's statement about the need for a spiritual dimension in one's life?

2. As Isabel leaves the hospital after being sickened by eating wild mushrooms, she stops and speaks to a young man who has attempted suicide. If you were in his position, how would you feel about Isabel's words with you? Is it intrusive to speak to him, or is it an important act of kindness?

3. Cat's new employee, Sinclair, is the sort of person Isabel can't get along with. What is at the heart of their conflict when they work together in the store? What does their interaction, and Isabel's annoyance with him, tell us about Isabel's ideals of human behavior?

4. Recalling a conversation with a friend who commented that in a country village people say good morning to strangers, Isabel thinks, "But we are not moral strangers to those we see in the street." Do you agree with Isabel's principle of "moral proximity"? How would life be different if most people thought about moral issues as Isabel does?

5. Visiting Rory Cameron's village, Isabel passes by some cows poking their head through a gate. "'I'm sorry, I have nothing for you,' she muttered." Then she thinks, "It's come to this at last: I'm talking to cows." How would you describe Isabel's sense of humor?

6. Isabel believes that Rory is not Jane's biological father, and that Alastair Rankeillor probably is. Catherine Succoth had suggested that Rory was the person Jane was looking for, but she confirms Isabel's hunch when they meet again and she apologizes for having been misleading. But now that Jane and Rory have struck up such a strong bond, Isabel doesn't know how to proceed. What is the right thing for Isabel to do in this situation?

7. When they next meet, Jane admits that Georgina told her that Rory cannot be her father, because he's infertile. Georgina hasn't told him the truth about why they haven't had children: "she decided to protect him from the psychological burden of the knowledge of his infertility." Given that Rory is a sensitive and disappointed man, are Georgina and Jane right in protecting him from the knowledge that Jane isn't his daughter?

FULL BODY BURDEN

Kristen Iverson

It's a book about the destructive power of secrets—both family and government. Her father's hidden liquor bottles, the strange cancers in children in the neighborhood, the truth about what was made at Rocky Flats (cleaning supplies, her mother guessed)—best not to inquire too deeply into any of it.

But as Iversen grew older, she began to ask questions. She learned about the infamous 1969 Mother's Day fire, in which a few scraps of plutonium spontaneously ignited and—despite the desperate efforts of firefighters—came perilously close to a "criticality," the deadly blue flash that signals a nuclear chain reaction. Intense heat and radiation almost melted the roof, which nearly resulted in an explosion that would have had devastating consequences for the entire Denver metro area. Yet the only mention of the fire was on page 28 of the *Rocky Mountain News*, underneath a photo of the Pet of the Week. In her early thirties, Iversen even worked at Rocky Flats for a time, typing up memos in which accidents were always called "incidents."

"One of the most important stories of the nuclear era—as personal and powerful as "Silkwood," told with the suspense and narrative drive of The Hot Zone.*" —***Rebecca Skloot, author of *The Immortal Life of Henrietta Lacks*

About the Author: **Kristen Iversen** grew up in Arvada, Colorado, near the Rocky Flats nuclear weaponry facility and received a Ph.D. in English from the University of Denver. She is director of the MFA Program in Creative Writing at the University of Memphis and editor-in-chief of *The Pinch*, an award-winning literary journal. She is also the author of *Molly Brown: Unraveling the Myth*, winner of the Colorado Book Award for Biography and the Barbara Sudler Award for Nonfiction. Iversen has two sons and lives in Memphis. Visit her website at KristenIversen.com.

June 2012 | Hardcover | Memoir | 416 pp | $25.00 | ISBN 9780307955630
Paperback available June 2013 (ISBN 9780307955654; $15.00)
Crown | randomhouse.com | kristeniversen.com
Also available as: eBook and Audiobook
Kristen loves to talk to Reader's Groups via phone, skype, or in person if her schedule permits. You can contact her at kristen@kristeniversen.com

CONVERSATION STARTERS

1. In this book, author Kristen Iversen weaves together two narratives: a memoir of growing up in Arvada and an historical account of Rocky Flats and the nuclear industry. What effect did moving back and forth between the two storylines have on your experience of reading the book? Did you find one of the two storylines more compelling than the other?

2. While horseback riding one day, Iversen is disturbed when she comes across a dead cow at the edge of the lake near her house, and she describes the mountains nearby as "a dark, heavy presence, a watching shadow." The discovery of the cow seems like an ominous portent. Are there other examples of foreshadowing in the book?

3. At one point, Kristen's mother takes the family to see a psychiatrist and each member of the family draws a picture of home. The passage reveals key elements of the family dynamic. What did you learn about each family member's coping mechanisms from this scene? In what different ways did Kristen and her siblings respond to their father's alcoholism and to the secrets of Rocky Flats as they were revealed over time?

4. Immediately after Kristen learns that Mark has died, her parents argue and then her father knocks on her bedroom door. "How can I let him in when a thousand times he has cast me out?" she asks herself, and she does not let him in. Do you think she was right to protect herself from her father?

5. During the Cold War, an impenetrable veil existed between the nuclear weapons industry and the general public. The U.S. government considered this secrecy necessary for national security. Do you think there is any way the government could have communicated more to the general public without jeopardizing the nation's safety?

6. For many years the nuclear weapons industry was exempted from environmental regulation because national defense was considered a higher priority. This book reveals the tragic consequences of that exemption. Are there situations in which you believe it is justified to exempt the government, certain industries, or private companies from the law?

7. Do you live near a nuclear site or nuclear power plant? If so, has your state or local government informed you of the potential risks of living near such a facility, or about emergency response plans in the event of a serious accident involving radioactive contamination?

THE GILDER
Kathryn Kay

In Marina Nesmith's skilled hands, even the most tarnished picture frame or object d'art can be made perfect once again. Her life, too, seems flawless, at least on the surface. But more and more, Marina is conscious of what she lacks—someone to share her joys and sorrows with, confidence in the decisions she's made, and the courage to tell her teenage daughter, Zoe, the truth about her father.

Then Marina is invited to return to Florence, where she lived years before while learning her trade as a gilder. In those heady days, she wandered the city's picturesque streets, marveling at the masterpieces in the Duomo and the Pitti Palace. In the church of Santa Croce, she met Thomas, an American photographer who, along with his wife Sarah, introduced Marina to a thrilling, bohemian world of art and beauty. Through them, she also learned about love, lies, and the way one mistake can multiply into many. Now, as her past and present collide, Marina will finally have to move beyond the intricate veneer she's crafted around herself, and find the life that she—and Zoe—have been looking for.

"The Gilder engages the reader from the very first line. Amid sensuous details of life and art in Florence, Kathryn Kay tells a compelling story of seduction and betrayal which ultimately transforms into a story of love and redemption." —**Holly Chamberlin, author of *Summer Friends***

"After reading Kathryn Kay's lovely debut, I had the best kind of cry. What a beautiful, emotional novel. I loved the way she writes about love, necessary secrets, and the dark unknowability of another person, no matter how close. She writes so well about the vulnerability of strong women, the complexity of long friendship, the ways mothers and daughters protect each other, and sweet, tender forgiveness." — **Luanne Rice, *New York Times* bestselling author**

ABOUT THE AUTHOR: Following college, **Kathryn Kay** spent five years living in Florence, Italy, where she studied restoration and gilding. Kathryn is the founder of the Nantucket Writers Studio, which offers writing workshops for women. She has three adult children, and lives on Nantucket Island with her husband, Robert.

January 2012 | Trade Paperbacks | Fiction | 320 pp | $15.00 | ISBN 978075826223
Kensington Books | kensingtonbooks.com | kathrynkay.com
Also available as: eBook

CONVERSATION STARTERS

1. The novel's title, *The Gilder*, refers to Marina's profession. In what ways does the concept of "gilding" become a subtext of the story?

2. In what ways does Marina's youth influence her attraction to Sarah and Thomas and her initial experience in Florence? Did her upbringing make her more sophisticated or more naïve?

3. What does Marina learn about Thomas when she first attends his photography show? How do you think she feels about what she discovers?

4. To what extent was Marina culpable in being seduced by Thomas? At what point in the story did the seduction begin?

5. Marina did not tell Sarah about being seduced by Thomas for fear it would damage their friendship irreparably. When she discovered she was pregnant, do you think she should have told Sarah and Thomas? Was there another point in time at which she could have told them about Zoe?

6. What was the basis for Marina's attraction to Sarah? Did Sarah play with Marina's feelings intentionally? Was Marina a lesbian/bisexual or simply a woman who fell in love with her best friend? Do you think Sarah loved Marina in a way she was unable to accept?

7. Was Marina right not to tell Zoe the truth about her father's identity? How much of the truth should she have shared with Zoe?

8. To what extent does Marina use her work and her daughter as an excuse for not allowing herself a personal life?

9. After Zoe's birth, Marina's life is closely linked with that of Lydia and June. Why did the author create a lesbian couple to befriend Marina?

10. Marina vacillated greatly about whether to tell Sarah the truth when she returned to Florence as a grown woman. If Marina had not stumbled upon the bust in Sarah's studio, do you think she would have told Sarah the truth?

11. Do you think that Sarah sending the camera to Zoe at the end of the book indicates she will forgive Marina? Is it conceivable that a person might be able to forgive such a betrayal?

GONE GIRL

By Gillian Flynn

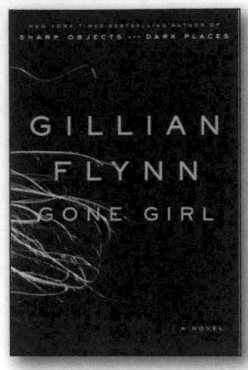

On a warm summer morning in North Carthage, Missouri, it is Nick and Amy Dunne's fifth wedding anniversary. Presents are being wrapped and reservations are being made when Nick's clever and beautiful wife disappears from their rented McMansion on the Mississippi River. Husband-of-the-Year Nick isn't doing himself any favors with cringe-worthy daydreams about the slope and shape of his wife's head, but passages from Amy's diary reveal the alpha-girl perfectionist could have put anyone dangerously on edge. Under mounting pressure from the police and the media—as well as Amy's fiercely doting parents—the town golden boy parades an endless series of lies, deceits, and inappropriate behavior. Nick is oddly evasive, and he's definitely bitter—but is he really a killer?

As the cops close in, every couple in town is soon wondering how well they know the one that they love. With his twin sister, Margo, at his side, Nick stands by his innocence. Trouble is, if Nick didn't do it, where is that beautiful wife? And what was in that silvery gift box hidden in the back of her bedroom closet?

"An irresistible summer thriller with a twisting plot worthy of Alfred Hitchcock. Burrowing deep into the murkiest corners of the human psyche, this delectable summer read will give you the creeps and keep you on edge until the last page." —People (**four stars**)

About the Author: **Gillian Flynn** is the author of *The New York Times* bestseller *Dark Places*, which was a *The New Yorker* Reviewers' Favorite, *Weekend* TODAY Top Summer Read, *Publishers Weekly* Best Book of 2009, and *Chicago Tribune* Favorite Fiction choice; and the Dagger Award winner *Sharp Objects*, which was an Edgar nominee for Best First novel, a BookSense pick, and a Barnes & Noble Discover selection. Her work has been published in twenty-eight countries. She lives in Chicago with her husband and son.

June 2012 | Hardcover | Fiction | 432 pp | $25.00 | ISBN 9780307588364
Crown | randomhouse.com | gillian-flynn.com
Also available as: eBook and Audiobook

Gillian Flynn's other **Reading Group Choices'** selections: *Dark Places* and *Sharp Objects*

CONVERSATION STARTERS

1. Do you like Nick or Amy? Did you find yourself picking a side? Do you think the author intends for us to like them? Why or why not?

2. Does the author intend for us to think of Nick or Amy as the stronger writer? Do you perceive one or the other as a stronger writer, based on their narration/journal entries? Why?

3. Do you think Amy and Nick both believe in their marriage at the outset?

4. What do you make of Nick's seeming paranoia on the day of his fifth anniversary, when he wakes with a start and reports feeling, *You have been seen*?

5. What is Go's role in the book? Why do you think the author wrote her as Nick's twin? Is she a likable character?

6. Is there some truth to Amy's description of the "dancing monkeys"— her friends' hapless partners who are forced to make sacrifices and perform "sweet" gestures to prove their love? How is this a counterpoint to the "cool girl"?

7. What do you think of Marybeth and Rand Elliott? Is the image they present sincere? What do you think they believe about Amy?

8. How does the book deal with the divide between perception and reality, or between public image and private lives? Which characters are most skillful at navigating this divide, and how?

9. While in hiding, Amy begins to explore what the "real" Amy likes and dislikes. Do you think this is a true exploration of her feelings, or is she acting out yet another role? In these passages, what does she mean when she refers to herself as "I" in quotes?

10. What do you think of Amy's quizzes—and "correct" answers—that appear throughout the book? As a consistent thread between her *Amazing Amy* childhood and her adult career, what does her quiz-writing style reveal about Amy's true personality and her understanding of the world?

11. Do Nick and Amy have friends? Consider Nick's assurance that Noelle was deluded in her claims of friendship with Amy, and also the friends described in Amy's journal. How "real" are these friendships? What do you think friendship means to each of them?

12. Do you believe Amy truly would have committed suicide? Why does she return?

13. Were you satisfied with the book's ending? What do you think the future holds for Nick, Amy, and their baby boy?

GRACE

T. Greenwood

Every family photograph hides a story. Some are suffused with warmth and joy, others reflect the dull ache of disappointed dreams. For thirteen-year-old Trevor Kennedy, taking photos helps make sense of his fractured world. His father, Kurt, struggles to keep a business going while also caring for Trevor's aging grandfather, whose hoarding has reached dangerous levels. Trevor's mother, Elsbeth, all but ignores her son while doting on his five-year-old sister, Gracy, and pilfering useless drugstore items.

Trevor knows he can count on little Gracy's unconditional love and his art teacher's encouragement. None of that compensates for the bullying he has endured at school for as long as he can remember. But where Trevor once silently tolerated the jabs and name-calling, now anger surges through him in ways he's powerless to control.

Only Crystal, a store clerk dealing with her own loss, sees the deep fissures in the Kennedy family—in the haunting photographs Trevor brings to be developed, and in the palpable distance between Elsbeth and her son. And as their lives become more intertwined, each will be pushed to the breaking point, with shattering, unforeseeable consequences.

"Harrowing, heartfelt and ultimately so realistically human in its terror and beauty it may haunt you for days after you finish it." —San Diego Union-Tribune

ABOUT THE AUTHOR: **T. Greenwood** is the author of seven novels, including *Two Rivers* and *The Hungry Season*. She has received numerous grants for her writing, including a National Endowment for the Art Literature Fellowship and a grant from the Maryland State Arts Council. *Two Rivers* was named Best General Fiction Book at the San Diego Book Awards in 2010, and five of her novels have been BookSense76/IndieBound picks. Greenwood is originally from Vermont, but now lives with her family in San Diego, California, where she teaches creative writing and studies photography.

April 2012 | Trade Paperback | Fiction | 352 pp | $15.00 | ISBN 9780758250926
Kensington Books | kensingtonbooks.com | tgreenwood.com
Also available as: eBook

CONVERSATION STARTERS

1. When Crystal first goes to the Kennedys' house, she observes: "What you see on the outside rarely reflects what's really on the inside. She, of all people, understood that appearances can be deceiving." Discuss the idea of perception in this novel. Compare Crystal's assumptions of the Kennedy family through the photos and her interactions with Elsbeth and Gracy with each of the characters' own narratives. Do you think her view of them is accurate at all? Talk about Elsbeth's and Kurt's opposite reactions to Trevor's pictures of Gracy. Further, consider how your life might look to an outsider and how accurate that perception is or how it differs from the truth.

2. Discuss the various father-son relationships: Kurt and Trevor, Jude and Kurt, Jude and Billy. Are there patterns to be found? Any broken? How is Kurt like his father? How is he different? What parallels are there between the opening scene and the one in which Jude catches Billy with a man in the junk-yard?

3. Trevor is a victim of Ethan and Mike's bullying, but is he also victimized by those people who fail to protect him? Who do you believe is at fault for the way he is treated? How do you think he handled the bullying? Should he have fought more, reported it, ignored it? What could have been done to protect him and other students?

4. Talk about the theme of stealing in *Grace*. Elsbeth shoplifts, Trevor steals equipment and chemicals from school, and Crystal steals Gracy. What else is stolen, figuratively and literally, over the course of the novel?

5. Photography allows Trevor to see the world as an artist. Does this make his world more endurable to him? What impact does art—in the form of photography, drawing, tattoos, etc.—have on each of the characters in *Grace*?

6. Why is Crystal so consumed by Elsbeth and Grace? How does her relationship with the Kennedys change her? Did this event actually, in the end, help her get over the loss of her own Grace or make her more regretful?

7. Discuss Elsbeth's feelings regarding Trevor and Gracy. Do you believe it's possible for a mother to love one child more than another for no reason? Are she and Kurt bad parents? Why or why not?

8. Discuss the concept of grace in this novel. Think about all of the definitions and uses of the word.

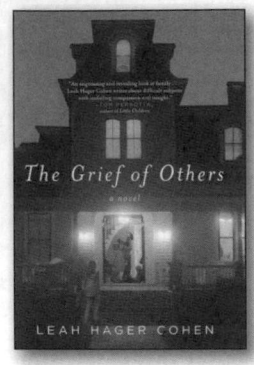

THE GRIEF OF OTHERS

By Leah Hager Cohen

In the tradition of *The Memory Keeper's Daughter*, a gripping, generous, and provocative novel chronicling the grief that follows the death of a newborn—and leads to a family's emotional reawakening.

Unable to express their grief over the loss of their newborn baby, John and Ricky Ryrie struggle to regain a semblance of normalcy for themselves and for their two older children. They pretend not only that little has changed, but that their marriage and their family have always been intact. Yet long suppressed uncertainties about their relationship come roiling to the surface, and a dreadful secret emerges with unexpected reverberations.

"Cohen creates gorgeous, uncommon descriptions that sound like grace notes on her pages . . . There's pain in reading this book, but there's another thread running through it, too, gleaming with all the vibrancy of Cohen's prose: hope." —The Washington Post

"Leah Hager Cohen is one of our foremost chroniclers of the mundane complexities, nuanced tragedies, and unexpected tenderness of human connection." —The New York Times Book Review

ABOUT THE AUTHOR: **Leah Hager Cohen** is the author of four nonfiction books, including *Train Go Sorry* and *Glass, Paper, Beans*, and three novels, most recently *House of Lights*. Four of her books have been named Notable Books of the Year by *The New York Times*. She is a frequent contributor to *The New York Times Book Review* and lives in Belmont, MA.

September 2012 | Trade Paperback | Fiction | 400 pp | $16.00 | ISBN 9781594486128
Riverhead Books | us.penguingroup.com | leahhagercohen.com
Also available as: eBook

CONVERSATION STARTERS

1. The book's prologue opens with the physical description of a beautiful newborn baby and his mother's intimate emotional connection to him, despite what she knows of his fate. What does the author achieve with this opening? Did it make you more invested in the plight of the mother, or the loss of the baby? Did it affect your feelings about the mother later in the book, when you gained a fuller understanding of what led up to this point?

2. Eventually, it is revealed that Ricky kept something deeply important from her husband. What do you think of her decision? How do you think you would have acted in that situation?

3. When her husband learns the truth about what Ricky has kept from him, he equates it with infidelity. What do you think? How does Ricky's deceit compare to having an affair?

4. John and Ricky try very hard to be good parents. Why don't they notice how much their children are suffering? What opens their eyes finally? How do they try to correct their behavior?

5. Think about times when you yourself have grieved. Which Ryrie did you behave the most like? How did you move past that time of loss?

6. The author herself says that her inspiration for this book came from her own miscarriage. Think about the types of losses that people are encouraged to keep to themselves or "get over." How does that grief get expressed? Would it be healthier if there were more public acknowledgment of that grief?

7. In addition to the main narrative, there are substantial flashbacks in the novel, including the lake vacation one. Why do you think the author chose to tell these parts of the story?

8. Think about grief itself. We often try to stigmatize it as a dark emotion that should not be indulged. How is grief good for a person? A family? What is the benefit of sharing?

THE HARE WITH AMBER EYES

The Hidden Inheritance

By Edmund de Waal

Edmund de Waal is a world-famous ceramicist. Having spent thirty years making beautiful pots —which are then sold, collected, and handed on—he has a particular sense of the secret lives of objects. When he inherited a collection of 264 tiny Japanese wood and ivory carvings, called netsuke, he wanted to know who had touched and held them, and how the collection had managed to survive.

And so begins this extraordinarily moving memoir and detective story as de Waal discovers both the story of the netsuke and of his family, the Ephrussis, over five generations. A nineteenth-century banking dynasty in Paris and Vienna, the Ephrussis were as rich and respected as the Rothchilds. Yet by the end of the World War II, when the netsuke were hidden from the Nazis in Vienna, this collection of very small carvings was all that remained of their vast empire.

"A family memoir written with a grace and modesty that almost belie the sweep of its contents: Proust, Rilke, Japanese art, the rue de Monceau, Vienna during the Second World War. The most enchanting history lesson imaginable." — The New Yorker

"An extraordinary history . . . A wondrous book, as lustrous and exquisitely crafted as the netsuke at its heart." —The Christian Science Monitor

ABOUT THE AUTHOR: **Edmund de Waal**'s porcelain has been displayed in many museum collections around the world, and he has recently made an installation for the dome of the Victoria and Albert Museum. He was apprenticed as a potter, studied in Japan, and studied English at Cambridge. He is Professor of Ceramics at the University of Westminster and lives in London with his family.

August 2011 | Trade Paperback | Memoir | 368 pp | $16.00 | ISBN 9780312569372
Picador | us.macmillian.com | edmunddewaal.com
Also available as: eBook and Audiobook

CONVERSATION STARTERS

1. Charles, like the rest of Paris, became swept up in the fad of "japonisme," which led to the original purchase of the netsuke. What did these objects represent to their collectors in the Belle Epoque?

2. In addition to his passion for Durer and the Old Masters and Japanese art, Charles radically embraced the Impressionists. What did he love about that new style? Which of these art spheres seems most quintessentially "Charles"?

3. Did you develop any new impressions of the major French art figures— Degas, Renoir, Proust—in light of their interaction with Charles?

4. How did the relationship between collector, patron, and artist evolve from Charles's Paris to Viktor's Vienna to Iggie's Tokyo? Where does Edmund fall in these roles?

5. The word "insatiability" was used by anti-Semites as a way to propagandize against Jewish families' material success. Why does this word become such a slur? How might the term apply more positively to collectors of things—and stories?

6. Why did Charles give away his beloved netsuke to Viktor and Emmy?

7. Edmund remarks on the coldness and lack of texture in the Palais at Vienna. What do the differences between Charles's salon in Paris and Viktor's grand Palais say about the two men?

8. Do you agree with Edmund's assessment that the netsuke need not go back to Japan; that their travels and stories have given them an identity of their own?

9. The Ephrussi patriarch had a vision for his family, but it was dependent upon the future generations' aptitude and willingness. How do the Ephrussi childrens' responses to their "calling" vary? How does Edmund's book fit into the Ephrussi legacy?

10. You've likely read many accounts of Nazi raid and Jewish persecution at the start of the occupation, but did anything surprise you or stand out in this account of the takeover of the Palais?

11. Viktor and Emmy received vague warnings about the coming threats and were encouraged to flee their home. Would you have been able to walk away from such history and treasures without knowing what was ahead?

12. Viktor essentially sacrificed the Ephrussi dynasty for the sake of his new home country, Austria. Do you think anti-Semetic pressure drove him to become a perfectly loyal citizen, or did Viktor's allegiance represent his true feeling?

13. Why do you think Iggie renounced his American citizenship?

HEMINGWAY'S GIRL

By *Erika Robuck*

In Depression-era Key West, Mariella Bennet, the daughter of an American fisherman and a Cuban woman, knows hunger. Her struggle to support her family following her father's death leads her to a bar and bordello, where she bets on a risky boxing match . . . and attracts the interest of two men: world-famous writer, Ernest Hemingway, and Gavin Murray, one of the WWI veterans who are laboring to build the Overseas Highway.

When Mariella is hired as a maid by Hemingway's second wife, Pauline, she enters a rarified world of lavish, celebrity-filled dinner parties and elaborate off-island excursions. As she becomes caught up in the tensions and excesses of the Hemingway household, the attentions of the larger-than-life writer become a dangerous temptation . . . even as straightforward Gavin Murray draws her back to what matters most. Will she cross an invisible line with the volatile Hemingway, or find a way to claim her own dreams? As a massive hurricane bears down on Key West, Mariella faces some harsh truths . . . and the possibility of losing everything she loves.

"Robuck's breathtaking alchemy is to put us inside the world of Hemingway and his wife Pauline. . . . Dazzlingly written and impossibly moving, this novel is a supernova." —**Caroline Leavitt**, *The New York Times* **Bestselling Author of** *Pictures of You*

"Evokes a setting of the greatest fascination. . . . This is assured and richly enjoyable storetelling." —**Margaret Leroy, author of** *The Soldier's Wife*

ABOUT THE AUTHOR: **Erika Robuck** is a contributor to popular fiction blog, *Writer Unboxed*, and maintains her own blog called *Muse*. She is a member of The Hemingway Society and The Historical Novel Society, and lives in the Chesapeake Bay area with her husband and three sons.

September 2012 | Trade Paperback | Fiction | 352 pp | $16.00 | ISBN 9780451237880
New American Library | us.penguingroup.com | erikarobuck.com
Also available as: eBook

CONVERSATION STARTERS

1. At nineteen, Mariella tends to run with a rough crowd, and she indulges in behavior—drinking, gambling, petty theft—that would not have been considered lady-like during this time. Yet she holds fast to her own standards. Discuss her "moral code" and compare it to the moral code that the Hemingways and Gavin live by.
2. What do you think draws Mariella and Hemingway together? Do you think their relationship is more romantic or paternal, or something else?
3. What do you think about Mariella's conflicted feelings for Gavin and Hemingway? What are the differences and similarities in the way Mariella views each man? Why do you think Mariella and Gavin choose not to have sex until they're married?
4. Pauline is frequently angry and jealous over Hemingway's relationships with other women. Did you sympathize with her struggle to keep her husband's affections? Do you agree with Pauline's assertion that Hemingway's "only true love is his writing"?
5. The Key West community regards Hemingway with great respect and admiration, yet few of them know about his wild mood swings and tendency toward depression. How do you explain his emotional volatility? What do you think Jane Mason means when she says that Hemingway needs Mariella to be his friend?
6. Hemingway tells Mariella that he envies her poverty, claiming that he was "happy and true" when he was poor and living in Paris. What does this suggest about his current life in Key West?
7. Why does Mariella's family keep secret from her the fact that her father committed suicide? Does Mariella blind herself to the truth?
8. How did you feel about the treatment of World War I veterans at the Matecumbe work camps, and the veterans' propensity to drink and become violent? How does *Hemingway's Girl* portray attitudes by the government and the general population toward veterans during the 1930s?
9. Had you heard of the Labor Day hurricane, and its tragic consequences, before reading this novel? Compare the authorities' response to that devastating storm with the response of government officials to recent hurricanes and other natural disasters.
10. How does Erika Robuck's description of Key West in the 1930s compare to what you know of the island today?

HISTORY OF A PLEASURE SEEKER

By Richard Mason

The novel opens in Amsterdam at the turn of the last century. It moves to New York at the time of the 1907 financial crisis and proceeds onboard a luxury liner headed for Cape Town.

It is about a young man—Piet Barol—with an instinctive appreciation for pleasure and a gift for finding it. Piet's father is an austere administrator at Holland's oldest university. His mother, a singing teacher, has died—but not before giving him a thorough grounding in the arts of charm.

Piet applies for a job as tutor to the troubled son of Europe's leading hotelier: a child who refuses to leave his family's mansion on Amsterdam's grandest canal. As the young man enters this glittering world, he learns its secrets—and soon, quietly, steadily, finds his life transformed as he in turn transforms the lives of those around him.

*"Beautifully observed, perfectly paced, genuinely sexy, and in the end, a terrifically fun read. Mason's ability to inhabit the inner voices of the servants and those they serve lends the book a rich realism." —***The Boston Globe**

*"An engaging picaresque romp . . . funny, touching, and arousing. . . . Mason does a stellar job of creating a particular time and place." —***Edmonton Journal**

ABOUT THE AUTHOR: **Richard Mason** was born in South Africa in 1978 and lives in New York City. His first novel, *The Drowning People*, published when he was twenty-one and still a student at Oxford, sold more than a million copies worldwide and won Italy's Grinzane Cavour Prize for Best First Novel. He is also the author of *Natural Elements*, which was chosen by the *Washington Post* as one of the best books of 2009 and longlisted for the IMPAC Prize and the *Sunday Times* Literary Award. *History of a Pleasure Seeker* is his fourth novel.

November 2012 | Trade Paperback* | Fiction | 336 pp | $15.95 | ISBN 9780307949288
Vintage | randomhouse.com | richard-mason.org
Also available as: eBook
*Hardcover jacket pictured above.

CONVERSATION STARTERS

1. Who is the "pleasure seeker" of the title? Who else might that describe?
2. What is the metaphor of the tightrope?
3. How do the characters' different religious beliefs shape the events of the story?
4. "Like his father, Egbert was deeply private about his interior afflictions" (page 40). Are there other ways in which father and son are alike? How are they different?
5. Throughout the novel, Mason calls our attention to shared character traits. What do Egbert and Piet share? Piet and Maarten?
6. What role does guilt play in Piet's actions?
7. The voices Egbert hears are guided by color: "toying with primary colors was an offense that merited prolonged punishment" (page 100). Why do you think color affects Egbert this way? How does Mason use color with other characters?
8. What is the significance of the horseback-riding scene on pages 109–14? Why does it prompt Piet to carry Egbert outside?
9. How does having money—or not having it—affect the characters' behavior? What about the other members of the household staff? In the terms of this novel, what is the difference between money and class?
10. Why is Piet willing to risk everything to see Jacobina? Is he in love with her?
11. When Louisa seeks her father's help in opening a shop, he tells her: "You must marry a man with talent and ambition, whose interests you may serve as your mother has served mine. That is the way in which a woman may succeed." Is this true for all the women in the novel? How are things changing with the times?
12. What finally gives Egbert the strength to go outside on his own? What role does music play in the decision?
13. When Piet turns down Louisa's proposal, what is the result? How does it influence the novel's denouement?
14. Why doesn't the novel end when Piet leaves the Vermeulen-Sickerts household? How might you have imagined Piet's next steps, if Mason hadn't supplied them?
15. How does Piet's interlude with his father change your understanding of his character? How did his late mother shape his behavior?
16. What role does Didier play in the novel's ending? What impact might a different response from him have had on Piet's future?

HOME

By Toni Morrison

America's most celebrated novelist, Nobel Prize-winner Toni Morrison extends her profound take on our history with this twentieth-century tale of redemption: a taut and tortured story about one man's desperate search for himself in a world disfigured by war.

Frank Money is an angry, self-loathing veteran of the Korean War who, after traumatic experiences on the front lines, finds himself back in racist America with more than just physical scars. His home may seem alien to him, but he is shocked out of his crippling apathy by the need to rescue his medically abused younger sister and take her back to the small Georgia town they come from and that he's hated all his life. As Frank revisits his memories from childhood and the war that have left him questioning his sense of self, he discovers a profound courage he had thought he could never possess again.

A deeply moving novel about an apparently defeated man finding his manhood—and his home.

"Gorgeous and intense, brutal yet heartwarming . . . like a slingshot that wields the impact of a missile. . . . Home is as accessible, tightly composed and visceral as anything Morrison has written. . . . [Her] shorter, more direct sentences have the capacity to leave a reader awestruck. . . . Devastating, deeply humane, ever-relevant." —**Heller McAlpin, NPR**

About the Author: **Toni Morrison** is the author of ten novels, from *The Bluest Eye* (1970) to *A Mercy* (2008). She has received the National Book Critics Circle Award and the Pulitzer Prize. In 1993 she was awarded the Nobel Prize in Literature. She lives in New York.

January 2013 | Trade Paperback* | Fiction | 160 pp | $15.00 | ISBN 9780307740915
Vintage | randomhouse.com
*Hardcover jacket pictured above.

CONVERSATION STARTERS

1. Why has Toni Morrison chosen *Home* for her title? In what ways is the novel about both leaving home and coming home? What does home mean for Frank, for Cee, for Lenore, for Lily?

2. The race of the characters is not specified in the novel. How does Morrison make clear which characters are black and which are white? Why might she have chosen not to identify characters explicitly by their race?

3. What is the effect of alternating between Frank's first-person (italicized) narration and the third-person omniscient narration through which most of the story is told? What is the implied relationship between Frank and the narrator?

4. Talking about the horrors of war in Korea, Frank tells the reader: "You can't imagine it because you weren't there." Does the reader succeed in imagining it even though he or she was not there? How close to another's experience, even those radically unlike our own, can imagination take us?

5. How has Frank's war experience affected him? What symptoms of post-traumatic stress disorder does he exhibit? In what ways does he suffer from survivor guilt?

6. In what sense can *Home* be understood as Frank's confession?

7. Both Frank and Cee were eager to leave Lotus, Georgia, and never return. Why do they find it so comforting when they do go back? What is it about the place and people that feels to Frank "both fresh and ancient, safe and demanding" and makes Cee declare that this is where she belongs?

8. How have Miss Ethel and the other women in her community learned not just to live with, but to rise above, the limitations imposed on them? What moral code do they live by?

9. The flowering lotus is a plant of extraordinary beauty, but it is rooted in the muck at the bottom of ponds. In what ways is the fictional town of Lotus, Georgia, like a lotus plant?

10. Why is it important that Frank does not resort to violence against Dr. Beau? In what ways has Frank been changed by the experiences he undergoes in the novel?

11. Much has been written about racism in America. What does *Home* add to our understanding of the suffering blacks endured during the late 1940s and early 1950s? What is most surprising, and distressing, about the story Morrison tells?

THE HOUSE GIRL
By Tara Conklin

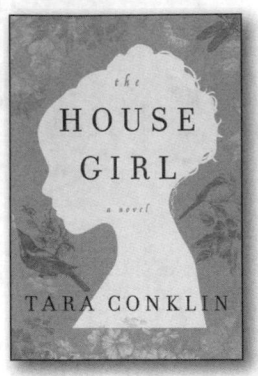

Lina Sparrow, an ambitious first-year associate in a lucrative Manhattan law firm, is given a difficult, highly sensitive assignment that can make her career: find the "perfect plaintiff" to lead a historic class-action lawsuit worth trillions of dollars in reparations for descendants of American slaves.

An unexpected lead comes from her father, renowned artist Oscar Sparrow, who tells her about a controversy currently rocking the art world. Art historians now suspect that the revered paintings of Lu Anne Bell, an antebellum artist known for her humanizing portraits of slaves from her plantation Bell Creek, were actually the work of her house slave, Josephine. A descendant of Josephine's would be the perfect face for the firm's lawsuit—if Lina can find one. But nothing is known about Josephine's fate following Lu Anne Bell's death in 1852. Did Josephine die at Bell Creek? Was she sold? Or did she escape? Searching for clues in old letters and plantation records, Lina begins to piece together Josephine's story—a journey that leads her to question her own life, including the full story of her mother's mysterious death twenty years before.

ABOUT THE AUTHOR: **Tara Conklin** has worked as a litigator in the New York and London offices of a major corporate law firm but now devotes her time to writing fiction. She received a BA in history from Yale University, a JD from New York University School of Law, and a Master of Law and Diplomacy from the Fletcher School (Tufts University). Tara Conklin's short fiction has appeared in the *Bristol Prize Anthology* and the *Pangea International Anthology*. Born in St. Croix, she grew up in Massachusetts and now lives with her family in Seattle, Washington.

February 2013 | Hardcover | Fiction | 384 pp | $25.99 | ISBN 9780062207395
William Morrow | harpercollins.com
Also available as: eBook and Audiobook

CONVERSATION STARTERS

1. As a servant in the Bell's home Josephine is literally "The House Girl." But how does this title also apply to Lina's character? What is the significance of Lina leaving her father's house at the close of the story?

2. The definition of "family" is unclear in this story: Lina's mother is absent for all of her life, Josephine's son is fathered by her married master. As Lina reflects on her mother's artwork she wonders whether you can create family connections: "What is blood and what is decision?" What is your response?

3. Separated by more than two centuries, Lina and Josephine's characters never meet, but Conklin's narrator tells this story through each of their perspectives. What similarities do you find between these two women? What would each character be able to teach the other?

4. On an empty page in her favorite book, Grace Sparrow writes "who is free?" We know that Josephine, Lottie and the others at the Bell plantation are literally enslaved. But who else experiences a lack of freedom in this story? Do you think these characters achieve freedom by the close of the novel?

5. Lu Anne Bell's relationship to Josephine is intense. She allows this slave, who gave birth to a boy fathered by her own husband, to remain in their home. She shares the most intimate moments of vulnerability with her when her illness is at its worst. But how does Josephine feel towards Lu Anne? How does she perceive her role in Lu Anne's life?

6. Josephine "keeps" her memories in Mr. Jefferson's chest of drawers. How is this similar to Oscar's paintings of Grace? How do these characters confront the loss and pain they've experienced? How do they hide things away?

7. Josephine is shocked to learn that the son she gave birth to at age fourteen survived and lives on a nearby farm. But even with this knowledge she decides to run alone. What do you make of this decision? Did she make this choice out of selfishness, a mother's love or something else entirely?

8. In the final pages of the novel, Lina decides to call her mother, asking Jasper to dial the phone number. What do you think Lina will say? Is she ready to build a relationship? Has she forgiven her mother for leaving?

IN THE GARDEN OF BEASTS
By Erik Larson

The time is 1933, the place, Berlin, when William E. Dodd becomes America's first ambassador to Hitler's Germany in a year that proved to be a turning point in history.

A mild-mannered professor from Chicago, Dodd brings along his wife, son, and flamboyant daughter, Martha. At first Martha is entranced by the parties and pomp, and the handsome young men of the Third Reich with their infectious enthusiasm for restoring Germany to a position of world prominence. Enamored of the "New Germany," she has one affair after another, including with the suprisingly honorable first chief of the Gestapo, Rudolf Diels. But as evidence of Jewish persecution mounts, confirmed by chilling first-person testimony, her father telegraphs his concerns to a largely indifferent State Department back home. Dodd watches with alarm as Jews are attacked, the press is censored, and drafts of frightening new laws begin to circulate. As that first year unfolds and the shadows deepen, the Dodds experience days full of excitement, intrigue, romance—and ultimately, horror, when a climactic spasm of violence and murder reveals Hitler's true character and ruthless ambition.

"By far his best and most enthralling work of novelistic history. . . . Powerful, poignant . . . a transportingly true story." —The New York Times

"Highly compelling. . . . Larson brings Berlin roaring to life in all its glamour and horror. . . . A welcome new chapter in the vast canon of World War II."
—Christian Science Monitor

About the Author: **Erik Larson** is the bestselling author of the National Book Award finalist and Edgar Award–winning *The Devil in the White City*. He lives in Seattle with his wife, three daughters, and a dog named Molly.

May 2012 | Trade Paperback | Nonfiction | 480 pp | $16.00 | ISBN 9780307408853
Broadway | randomhouse.com | eriklarson.com
Also available as: eBook and Audiobook
For a signed bookplate, please email rgc@randomhouse.com.

CONVERSATION STARTERS

1. In his prologue ("Das Vorspiel"), Erik Larson writes, "There are no heroes here, at least not of the Schindler's List variety, but there are glimmers of heroism." What heroism did you find in this history? Who were the greatest cowards?

2. Discuss the significance of the title, derived from a literal translation of the word Tiergarten. What is captured in the deceptive beauty of the garden, a refuge for many of the men and women described in the book? What does it take to transform a beautiful creature into a "beast"?

3. How was Martha able to appear youthful, even virginal, yet also sophisticated? What made her attractive to such a broad variety of men, from literary figures to military leaders? What type of man was she most attracted to?

4. Studying for his doctorate thesis in Leipzig, Dodd researched American history while he was a student far from his homeland. Returning to Germany decades later, what did he discover about his homeland by looking at it as an outsider?

5. Was Dodd's lack of wealth a help or a hindrance as an ambassador, especially in a time of economic depression? Would Hitler have been more intimidated by an American ambassador who lived lavishly?

6. Dodd was repeatedly reminded that his big-gest concern should be whether Germany would default on its massive debt to the United States. Why didn't Washington link Messersmith's warnings to America's economic interests? Do economic concerns still overshadow human rights in foreign policy today? Are economics and human rights dependent on each other?

7. *In the Garden of Beasts* captures the years when outsiders refused to believe Hitler was anything more than a passing sideshow. Dodd even sympathized with Hitler's belief that the Versailles Treaty gave Germany a raw deal, and that American banks were charging Germany unfair interest rates. Without the benefit of hindsight, what would you have believed about the political situation in Germany in the early 1930s?

8. How was it possible for Dodd and Messersmith to have such different perceptions of the same circumstances?

9. Discuss Martha's relationship with Boris. What allure did the Soviet Union have for her? Why was she drawn to travel there?

10. Discuss the Dodds' evolving attitudes toward Jews. Would you have hesitated to protect the Panofsky family (the Dodds' landlords)?

KEEPSAKE

By Kristina Riggle

Trish isn't perfect. She's divorced and raising two kids—so of course her house isn't pristine. But she's got all the important things right and she's convinced herself that she has it all under control. That is, until the day her youngest son gets hurt and Child Protective Services comes calling. It's at that moment when Trish is forced to consider the one thing she's always hoped wasn't true: that she's living out her mother's life as a compulsive hoarder.

The last person Trish ever wanted to turn to for help is her sister, Mary—meticulous, perfect Mary, whose house is always spotless . . . and who moved away from their mother to live somewhere else, just like Trish's oldest child has. But now, working together to get Trish's disaster of a home into livable shape, two very different sisters are about to uncover more than just piles of junk, as years of secrets, resentments, obsessions, and pain are finally brought into the light.

"A sensitive portrayal of a dysfunctional family struggling to make peace with their pasts. . . . Highly recommended." —Booklist (**starred review**)

About the Author: A freelance journalist, published short-story writer, and fiction coeditor at the e-zine Literary Mama, **Kristina Riggle** lives and writes in Grand Rapids, Michigan, with her husband, two kids, and dog.

July 2012 | Trade Paperback | Fiction | 384 pp | $14.99 | ISBN 9780062003072
William Morrow Paperbacks | harpercollins.com | kristinariggle.net
Also available as: eBook

CONVERSATION STARTERS

1. Before reading *Keepsake*, what did you know about hoarding, and the mental and emotional issues behind it? Do you know someone who hoards?
2. Have you watched documentary TV about people who hoard? Do you find these shows to be educational, and do you believe they genuinely help the subjects of the programs? What about the viewers at home? Do you think Trish would have recognized herself if she'd watched a show about hoarding?
3. Talk about Trish and Mary. Do you relate to either of the sisters, or both? If so, how?
4. What is your relationship with your own "stuff"? Are you like Trish, in that you might keep things you never use or buy unnecessary things in order to make yourself feel better? Or are you like Mary, in that clutter jangles your nerves and dirt upsets you?
5. Why do you think the sisters responded so differently to their upbringing by a hoarder parent? Why do you think Mary left to live with their father, while Trish stayed with their mother through the end of her adolescence?
6. In what ways is hoarding similar to a substance addiction?
7. Do you think Frances had a genuine choice in whether to keep her baby, or did the culture she lived in force her hand?
8. How different would their lives have been if Frances had kept her baby? Would Frances still have hoarded? Would Mary and Trish even have existed, or would keeping the baby have altered Frances's life so much that she never would have married the man she did?
9. Both Trish and her mother had husbands leave them because of their hoarding. Do you understand why they left? Could they have done anything to prevent what eventually happened to their wives?
10. In what ways is Mary's obsession with neatness connected to her discomfort with emotional closeness?
11. Discuss Seth and Mary's relationship. Why did Seth not initially think of Mary in a romantic way? Do you believe Mary can break down her emotional walls long enough to connect with Seth?
12. Will Trish ever let go of the crib? Do you believe it's harmful that she kept it? Have you hung on to something for reasons that you can't fully explain?
13. After reading *Keepsake*, do you have a deeper understanding about what makes someone hoard?

LAST SUMMER

Holly Chamberlin

The town of Yorktide, close to Maine's beautiful beaches and the city of Portland, seems like the perfect place to raise a family. For Jane Patterson, there's another advantage: her best friend, Frannie Giroux, lives next door, and their teenaged daughters, Rosie and Meg, are inseparable. But in the girls' freshman year of high school, everything changes.

Jane always felt lucky that she was able to work from home, to be there to nurture and protect Rosie. But has she been too protective? Rosie—quiet, shy, and also very pretty—attracts the sneers and slights of a clique of older girls. Over time, the bullying worsens. When Meg betrays their friendship, fearful that she too will be targeted, Rosie suffers an emotional breakdown.

Blaming both Meg and Frannie, Jane tries to help Rosie heal while dealing with her own guilt and anger. In the months that follow, each struggles with the ideas of forgiveness and compassion, of knowing when a friendship has been shattered beyond repair—and when hope can be salvaged, one small moment at a time . . .

"Chamberlin is pitch-perfect in her depiction of Rosie and Meg struggling to grow up, love, and forgive themselves and each other." —Publishers Weekly

"A timely tale of the impact of bullying on the victim and her loved ones. Readers will appreciate this engaging character study as the four females struggle with their deepest fears that divides them at a time when they need each other." —Midwest Book Review

About the Author: **Holly Chamberlin** was born and raised in New York City. While other kids were playing in the park, she was in the library reading or scribbling stories. She earned a Bachelor's and a Masters degree in literature from New York University, after which she worked as an editor at several publishing houses for nine years. In 1996 she moved to Boston, married, and established first a career as a ghostwriter, and then a career as a novelist of her own fiction. In 2003 she and her husband moved to Maine.

July 2012 | Trade Paperback | Fiction | 336 pp | $15.00 | ISBN 9780758235084
Kensington Books | kensingtonbooks.com | hollychamberlin.com
Also available as: eBook

CONVERSATION STARTERS

1. Talk about how Meg's perception of Rosie changes over the course of the story. For example, at one point Meg tells us she has always felt protective of Rosie. How does she come to realize that her friend has hidden reserves of strength?

2. Though she loves her mother, Meg is determined not to follow in her footsteps and wind up with a deadbeat ex-husband and struggling to make ends meet. Do you think Meg will succeed in her determination to go to college and build a successful career? Do you think she will be a happy woman?

3. Was Frannie wrong not to hide the extent of her ex-husband's poor character from her daughter? Or is brutal honesty best in such a situation? Do you think Frannie will be as open about Peter's character with her son when he reaches Meg's age? If not, why?

4. Jane loves her husband and feels very dependent upon him as the stronger and more courageous person in the relationship. And if not a particularly effusive man, Mike seems to be an attentive husband. Given what relatively little we know of it, what is your opinion of the Pattersons' marriage? If you could predict the future for Jane and Mike, what would it be?

5. In what circumstances would you read your child's private diary or journal? In what circumstances would you track her use of the Internet and social media services? The idea of privacy has changed enormously in the past few years. When, if ever, is it okay for a teacher or caregiver other than a parent to infringe upon a child's privacy?

6. Some people argue that no one deserves forgiveness, that it's a gift freely given by the one who has been wronged. Do you think that a person must accept the gift of forgiveness offered her and admit to feeling remorse in order for the "transaction" to be completed? Or is there really such a thing as "unilateral forgiveness"?

7. Traditionally, boys and girls have engaged in different types of harassment. In general, boys who bully feel the need to be powerful and in control; they take pleasure in the suffering of others. In general, girls who bully seek social dominance by excluding others from the network of friends. Talk about these differences. In what ways are male and female bullies similar?

LIFE OF PI
(Movie Tie-In)

By Yann Martel

After the sinking of a cargo ship, a solitary lifeboat remains bobbing on the wild blue Pacific. The only survivors from the wreck are a sixteen-year-old boy named Pi, a hyena, a wounded zebra, an orangutan—and a 450-pound royal bengal tiger. The scene is set for one of the most extraordinary and beloved works of fiction in recent years.

Universally acclaimed upon publication, *Life of Pi* is a modern classic.

"Life of Pi *could renew your faith in the ability of novelists to invest even the most outrageous scenario with plausible life.*" —*The New York Times Book Review*

A terrific book . . . Fresh, original, smart, devious, and crammed with absorbing lore.*" —**Margaret Atwood**

"*A story to make you believe in the soul-sustaining power of fiction.*" —*Los Angeles Times Book Review*

ABOUT THE AUTHOR: **Yann Martel** was born in Spain in 1963 of Canadian parents. After studying philosophy at university, he worked at odd jobs—tree-planter, dishwasher, security guard—and traveled widely before turning to writing at the age of twenty-six. He is the author of a collection of short stories; three novels, including the internationally acclaimed 2002 Man Booker Prize–winning novel *Life of Pi*, which spent fifty-seven weeks on the *New York Times* bestseller list, and *Beatrice and Virgil*; and a collection of letters to the Prime Minister of Canada, *What is Stephen Harper Reading?* Yann Martel lives in Saskatchewan, Canada.

October 2012 | Trade Paperback | 336 pp | $15.95 | ISBN 9780547848419
Houghton Mifflin Harcourt | hmhbooks.com
Also available as: eBook

CONVERSATION STARTERS

1. Pondicherry is described as an anomaly, the former capital of what was once French India. In terms of storytelling, what makes this town an appropriate choice for Pi's upbringing?
2. Yann Martel sprinkles the novel with italicized memories of the "real" Pi Patel and wonders in his author's note whether fiction is "the selective transforming of reality, the twisting of it to bring out its essence." If this is so, what is the essence of Pi?
3. What do you make of Pi's assertion at the beginning of chapter 16 that we are all "in limbo, without religion, until some figure introduces us to God"? Do you believe that Pi's piousness was a response to his father's atheism?
4. Among Yann Martel's gifts is a rich descriptive palette. Regarding religion, he observes the green elements that represent Islam and the orange tones of Hinduism. What color would Christianity be, according to Pi's perspective?
5. Besides the loss of his family and possessions, what else did Pi lose when the Tsimtsum sank? What did he gain?
6. Nearly everyone experiences a turning point that represents the transition from youth to adulthood, albeit seldom as traumatic as Pi's. What event marks your coming of age?
7. Why did Pi at first try so hard to save Richard Parker?
8. Pi imagines that his brother would have teasingly called him Noah. How does Pi's voyage compare to the biblical story of Noah, who was spared from the flood while God washed away the sinners?
9. Is *Life of Pi* a tragedy, romance, or comedy?
10. Do you agree with Pi's opinion that a zoo is more like a suburb than a jail?
11. How did you react to Pi's interview by the Japanese transport ministers? Did you ever believe that Pi's mother, along with a sailor and a cannibalistic cook, had perhaps been in the lifeboat with him instead of the animals? How does Yann Martel achieve such believability in his surprising plots?
12. The opening scene occurs after Pi's ordeal has ended. Discussing his work in the first chapter, Pi says that a necktie is a noose, and he mentions some of the things that he misses about India (in spite of his love for Canada). Would you say that this novel has a happy ending? How does the grown-up version of Pi contrast with his little-boy scenes?

LOVE ANTHONY
By Lisa Genova

Two women, each cast adrift by unforseen events in their lives, meet by accident on a Nantucket beach and are drawn into a friendship.

Olivia is a young mother whose eight-year-old severely autistic son has recently died. Her marriage badly frayed by years of stress, she comes to the island in a trial separation to try and make sense of the tragedy of her Anthony's short life.

Beth, a stay-at-home mother of three, is also recently separated after discovering her husband's long-term infidelity. In an attempt to recapture a sense of her pre-married life, she rekindles her passion for writing, determined to find her own voice again. But surprisingly, as she does so, Beth also finds herself channeling the voice of an unknown boy, exuberant in his perceptions of the world around him if autistic in his expression—a voice she can share with Olivia—(is it Anthony?)—that brings comfort and meaning to them both.

"Love Anthony broke my heart in the best way! I read it spellbound and breathless. If you don't know Lisa Genova's work already, meet your new favorite writer, storyteller, enchanter." —**Heidi W. Durrow, author of *The Girl Who Fell from the Sky*, Winner of the Bellwether Prize**

ABOUT THE AUTHOR: **Lisa Genova** graduated valedictorian from Bates College with a degree in biopsychology and holds a Ph.D. in neuroscience from Harvard University. She is a member of the Dementia Advocacy Support Network International and DementiaUSA and is an online columnist for the National Alzheimer's association. She lives with her husband and two children in Cape Cod. Her first two novels are *The New York Times* bestsellers *Still Alice* and *Left Neglected*.

September 2012 | Hardcover | Fiction | 320 pp | $26.00 | ISBN 9781439164686
Gallery | simonandschuster.com | lisagenova.com
Also available as: eBook and Audiobook

CONVERSATION STARTERS

1. How much did you know about this condition before starting *Love Anthony*? Do you know anyone who has autism or an autistic person in their family?

2. What significance does the setting of Nantucket play in this story? Would the story have been different if it had taken place in New York City or Chicago?

3. On the subject of marriage and fidelity, Beth's friend, Courtney, muses: "You're always at the mercy of the people you're in a relationship with, right?" Do you agree? What do you think of the advice she offers Beth?

4. Do you think the author accurately captured the voice of a young autistic boy in the *Anthony* chapters? Did these sections enhance Beth's story for you? What about Olivia's journal entries?

5. Toward the end of the story, Olivia has an epiphany when she realizes that "There was more to Anthony's life than his death. And there was more to Anthony than his autism." What do you think finally enables Olivia to have this realization? Was it a singular event or a process?

6. When Jimmy and Beth share their homework assignments given to them by Dr. Campbell, were you surprised by Beth's initial reaction? Why is forgiving Jimmy the one thing Beth can't do?

7. After reading Beth's novel, Olivia is convinced Anthony is speaking to her through Beth. Skeptical, Beth discusses the idea with the more spiritual Petra, who feels "we're all connected, even if we don't know how. Maybe communicating through you gives you the something you need in this lifetime." Do you agree or disagree with Petra?

8. Beth ultimately decides the lesson of her book is "Find someone to love and love without condition." Do you think this could also apply as an overall theme for *Love Anthony*? Can you find any others?

9. Which character did you relate to the most and why? Where do you see these characters in five years?

10. What do you think of Beth's epilogue? Do you think it provides a satisfying ending to her story? To the novel as a whole?

11. Another recurring theme of *Love Anthony* is faith—having faith, losing faith, and taking a leap of faith. Can you remember a time in your own life when you took a leap of faith?

MAINE

By J. Courtney Sullivan

For the Kellehers, Maine is a place where children run in packs, showers are taken outdoors, and old Irish songs are sung around a piano. As three generations of women arrive at the family's beach house, each brings her own hopes and fears. Maggie is thirty-two and pregnant, waiting for the perfect moment to tell her imperfect boyfriend the news; Ann Marie, a Kelleher by marriage, is channeling her domestic frustration into a dollhouse obsession and an ill-advised crush; Kathleen, the black sheep, never wanted to set foot in the cottage again; and Alice, the matriarch at the center of it all, would trade every floorboard for a chance to undo the events of one night, long ago.

By turns wickedly funny and achingly sad, *Maine* unveils the sibling rivalry, alcoholism, social climbing, and Catholic guilt at the center of one family, along with the abiding, often irrational love that keeps them coming back, every summer, to Maine and to each other.

"Sullivan presents women who may be stubborn and difficult, but she does so with such compassion and humor that we, too, end up rooting for them."
—Chicago Tribune

"[A] ruthless and tender novel about the way love can sometimes redeem even the most contentious of families. Like all first-rate comic fiction, Maine *uses humor to examine the truths of the heart, in New England and far beyond."*
—The Washington Post Book World

ABOUT THE AUTHOR: **J. Courtney Sullivan** is the author of *The New York Times* best-selling novel *Commencement*. Her writing has appeared in *The New York Times Book Review*, the *Chicago Tribune*, *New York*, *Elle*, *Glamour*, *Allure*, and *Men's Vogue*, among others. She lives in Brooklyn, New York.

May 2012 | Trade Paperback | Fiction | 528 pp | $15.95 | ISBN 9780307742216
Vintage | randomhouse.com | jcourtneysullivan.com
Also available as: eBook and Audiobook

CONVERSATION STARTERS

1. If you had to choose one word to describe the overriding theme of *Maine*, what would it be?
2. Which of the women in the novel would you say is a good mother, and why? Who resents motherhood the most?
3. What was Alice's motivation for changing her will? Why did she wait so long to tell her family?
4. Speaking of secrets, many of the characters in the novel keep substantial secrets for one reason or another. Whose is the most damaging?
5. What role does alcohol—and alcoholism—play in the novel? How do the characters use alcohol (or abstain from it)?
6. "Even after thirty-three years of marriage, Ann Marie sat at every family dinner and listened to them tell the same stories, over and over. She had never met a family so tied up in their own mythology." What is the mythology of the Kelleher family? Who is helped the most by it? And harmed the most?
7. After Daniel's funeral, Alice says to Kathleen, "You killed him, and now you want me dead too, is that it?" Why does she lash out like this?
8. Why did Daniel's death have such an impact on the family?
9. What did you think of the revelation about Mary's death? Was Alice right to blame herself?
10. Maggie says to Alice, "I actually want this baby. I don't feel it's a mistake the way you did with us." Why does Maggie feel this way about her mother?
11. Kathleen says to Alice, "News flash, Mom, you really weren't that talented. None of us stopped you from becoming anything. That was a stupid childish dream like everyone else has." How does this relate to Maggie's earlier outburst? How does the notion of sacrifice play into each woman's story about herself?
12. How did Ann Marie misread Steve so completely? And why does Kathleen's witnessing the event change her attitude toward Ann Marie? Why do you think Kathleen reacted the way she did?
13. Discuss the last lines of the book: "She prayed until she heard footsteps behind her, coming slowly down the aisle, a familiar voice softly calling out her name: 'Alice? Alice. It's time.'" Is this Father Donnelly, Daniel, or someone else? Which of these women would you like to spend more time with? Are there any you'd never want to see again?

THE MALICE OF FORTUNE

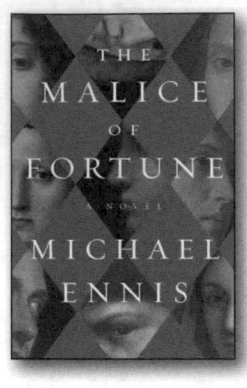

By Michael Ennis

A sweeping, intense historical thriller starring two of the great minds of Renaissance Italy: Niccolo Machiavelli and Leonardo da Vinci. Based on a real historical mystery, and involving serial murder and a gruesome cat and mouse game at the highest levels of the Church—it was the era of the infamous Borgias—*The Malice of Fortune* is a delicious treat for fans of Umberto Eco, Sarah Dunant, and Elizabeth Kostova.

This brilliant novel is an epic tale exploring the backdrop of the most controversial work of the Italian Renaissance, *The Prince*. Here, Niccolo Machiavelli, the great "scientist" of human behaviour becomes, in effect, the first criminal profiler, while his contemporary and sometime colleague, the erratic genius Leonardo da Vinci, brings his observational powers to the increasingly desperate hunt for a brilliant, terrifying serial murderer. Their foil and partner is the exquisite Damiata, scholar and courtesan. All three know their quarry is someone who holds enormous power, both to tear Italy apart, and destroy each of their most beloved dreams. And every thrilling step is based on historical fact.

"A true masterpiece . . . Michael Ennis has poured the knowledge and wisdom of many lifetimes into the exquisite form of a mystery so dark, so labyrinthine. The Malice of Fortune is stunning, terrifying, and utterly mesmerizing." —**Ann Fortier, author of *Juliet***

About the Author: **Michael Ennis** taught art history at the University of Texas, developed museum programs as a Rockefeller Foundation Fellow, and works as an independent curator and consultant. He has won several awards for art criticism, and written for such magazines as *Esquire* and *Architectural Digest*. His first historical novel, *Byzantium*; his second, *The Duchess of Milan*, was a Book-of-the-Month Club selection, and a History Book Club featured selection. Michael lives in Dallas with his wife, Ellen, and their Australian Shepherd, Zoë.

September 2012 | Hardcover | Fiction | 416 pp | $26.95 | ISBN 9780385536318
Doubleday | randomhouse.com
Also available as: eBook and Audiobook

....

CONVERSATION STARTERS

1. There is a marked consensus among Niccolo Machiavelli's modern biographers that few men were ever less "Machiavellian"—in the modern sense of the word—than Machiavelli himself. When you are introduced to the "real" Machiavelli in *The Malice of Fortune*, do you find his character surprising?

2. The setting of *The Malice of Fortune* is remarkably austere compared to the typical treatment of Renaissance Italy. What sort of mood did this setting establish? Can you compare *The Malice of Fortune* to other books with a similarly austere, forbidding setting?

3. In our time, do many people similarly share a loss of faith in ability of our institutions—financial institutions as well as government—to provide a stable society and insure fair opportunity for all as they do in *The Malice of Fortune*? Does Renaissance Italy provide a cautionary tale of the consequences when an entire people no longer believe that they have control over their lives?

4. Both Machiavelli and Leonardo are extraordinarily keen observers, yet their methods of observations are often at odds. How are they alike? How are they different?

5. Who would be more interesting to sit down and converse with today, Leonardo or Machiavelli? (Michael Ennis has a very strong opinion on this—which he'll be glad to share with your group!)

6. For all her acquired refinement and erudition, Damiata's origins are very lowly, and she must conceal the psychological scars of having been used by men—and women—for many years before she was able to govern her own fate. Can you cite examples where her rough edges and resentments are showing?

7. Machiavelli cautions that the innovation of the printing press is morally neutral, allowing lies to proliferate just as easily as truths. Would he issue the same warning to us, now that the internet and digital technology have brought about a second information revolution, with a similar democratization of knowledge?

8. In the *Malice of Fortune*, Machiavelli cautions us that the "new man" he has identified—what we would call a psychopath—has a nature that is particularly suited to attaining and holding political power. Some recent research has shown that psychopaths disproportionately occupy the highest offices in businesses and government today. Do you think that this sort of deeply flawed character is all too common among our corporate and political leaders?

THE MARRIAGE PLOT
By Jeffrey Eugenides

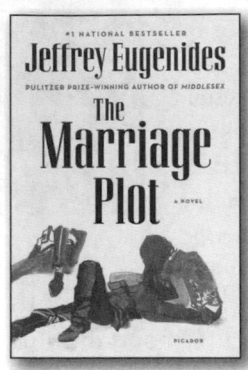

Are the great love stories of the nineteenth century dead? Or can there be a new story, written for today and alive to the realities of feminism, sexual freedom, prenups, and divorce?

It's the early 1980s. In American colleges, the wised-up kids are inhaling Derrida and listening to Talking Heads. But Madeleine Hanna, dutiful English major, is writing her senior thesis on Jane Austen and George Eliot, purveyors of the marriage plot that lies at the heart of the greatest English novels. As Madeleine studies the age-old motivations of the human heart, real life, in the form of two very different guys, intervenes—the charismatic and intense Leonard Bankhead, and her old friend the mystically inclined Mitchell Grammaticus. As all three of them face life in the real world they will have to reevaluate everything they have learned.

"Remind[s] us with uncommon understanding what it is to be young and idealistic, in pursuit of true love, and in love with books and ideas." —**Michiko Kakutani, *The New York Times***

"Wry, engaging, and beautifully constructed." —*The New York Times Book Review*

ABOUT THE AUTHOR: **Jeffrey Eugenides** was born in Detroit and attended Brown and Stanford Universities. His first novel, *The Virgin Suicides*, was published by FSG to great acclaim in 1993, and he has received numerous awards for his work. In 2003, Eugenides received the Pulitzer Prize for his novel *Middlesex* (FSG, 2002), which was also a finalist for the National Book Critics Circle Award, the International IMPAC Dublin Literary Award, and France's Prix Médicis.

September 2012 | Trade Paperback | Fiction | 496 pp | $16.00 | ISBN 9781250014764
Picador USA | us.macmillan.com
Also available as: eBook and Audiobook

CONVERSATION STARTERS

1. The opening scene features a litany of the books Madeleine loves. What were your first impressions of her, based on her library? How are her beliefs about love transformed throughout the novel?
2. When Phyllida fell in love with Alton, she gave up her dream of becoming an actress in Hollywood. What sustains the Hannas' marriage despite this sacrifice? How are Alwyn and Madeleine influenced by their parents' marriage? Is Alwyn's marriage to Blake a bad one?
3. Why is Madeleine more attracted to Leonard than to Mitchell? As she copes with Leonard's instability and her feelings of guilt, how does mental illness shape the relationship?
4. What does Mitchell hope to discover as a student of religion? What role does religion play in his quest to be loved? Is his ideal—a religion devoid of myth and artificial social structures—attainable?
5. What does sex mean to Madeleine, Leonard, and Mitchell? Over the course of the novel, what do they discover about fantasy versus reality and the tandem between physical and emotional satisfaction?
6. What recurring themes did you detect in Mitchell's trip overseas as he tries to manage his money, his love life, and Larry? Does he return to America a stronger, changed person or an amplified version of his college self?
7. Madeleine's parents are affluent and have enough free time to stay very involved in her life. Does this liberate her, or does it give her less freedom than Leonard, who is often left to fend for himself?
8. In their chosen career paths after college, what are Leonard and Madeleine each trying to uncover about life? Does his work on the yeast-cell experiment have anything in common with her work on Victorian novels?
9. Would you have said yes to Leonard's marriage proposal?
10. How does the novel's 1980s setting shape the plot? Do 21st-century college students face more or fewer challenges than Madeleine did?
11. Discuss the novel's meta-ending (an ending about endings). Does it reflect reality? What were your expectations for the characters?
12. Eugenides's previous fiction has given us unique, tragicomic perspectives on oppressive families, gender stereotypes, and the process of trying to discover our true selves. How does *The Marriage Plot* enhance your reading of Eugenides's other works?
13. Who did you become during your first year after college?

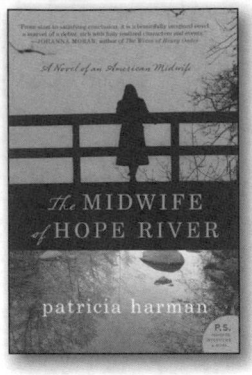

THE MIDWIFE OF HOPE RIVER

By Patricia Harman

Midwife Patience Murphy has a gift: a talent for escorting mothers through the challenges of bringing children into the world. Working in the hardscrabble conditions of Appalachia during the Depression, Patience takes the jobs that no one else wants, helping those most in need—and least likely to pay. She knows a successful midwifery practice must be built on a foundation of openness and trust—but the secrets Patience is keeping are far too intimate and fragile for her to ever let anyone in.

Honest, moving, and beautifully detailed, Patricia Harman's *The Midwife of Hope River* rings with authenticity as Patience faces nearly insurmountable difficulties. From the dangerous mines of West Virginia to the terrifying attentions of the Ku Klux Klan, Patience must strive to bring new light and life into an otherwise hard world.

"Midwives are warriors in this beautifully sweeping tale." **—Kirkus Reviews**

"A beautifully imagined novel, a marvel of a debut, rich with fully realized characters and events." **—Johanna Moran, author of *The Wives of Henry Oades***

About the Author: **Patricia Harman, CNM,** got her start as a lay midwife on rural communes and went on to become a nurse-midwife on the faculty of Ohio State University, Case Western Reserve University, and West Virginia University. She lives near Morgantown, West Virginia; has three sons; and is the author of two acclaimed memoirs. This is her first novel.

September 2012 | Trade Paperback | Fiction | 400 pp | $14.99 | ISBN 9780062198891
William Morrow Paperbacks | harpercollins.com | patriciaharman.com
Also available as: eBook

CONVERSATION STARTERS

1. The opening scene in *The Midwife of Hope River* presents a dark and scary view of birth. Do you think most women (and men) see birth that way, or do they look forward to childbirth as a peak experience? How do you feel about childbirth?

2. Have you ever lost a baby or known anyone who has?

3. Living without electricity was an ordinary part of rural life in the 1930s. We are so used to all our conveniences now. How would you feel about living without them?

4. Unions played a big part in Patience's life and an important part in U.S. history. What is your experience with unions? Have you ever been a union member, or has anyone in your family? What place do unions have in modern times?

5. Most people think of inhabitants of Appalachia as Caucasian. Did it surprise you to read about African-American miners?

6. What did you think about the developing friendship between Bitsy and Patience? Realistic? A stretch of the imagination?

7. Have you ever had a servant in your home? What was your relationship to them?

8. The author writes of Patience's loneliness, living out on the farm without Mrs. Kelly or her Pittsburgh community of radical friends. Do you think you could make it alone like that?

9. What do you think the book says about the human capacity to endure hardship, loneliness, and fear?

10. Patience tells us of her grief and guilt over having killed her husband accidentally while trying to get the goon off him at the Battle of Blair Mountain. The experience defined her life for many years, yet she couldn't talk about it. How can a person let go of something like that? How important is it for a person to find someone to talk to?

THE MOST DANGEROUS THING

By Laura Lippman

Years ago, they were all the best of friends. But as time passed and circumstances changed, they grew apart, became adults with families of their own, and began to forget about the past—and the terrible lie they all shared. But now Gordon ("Go-Go"), the youngest and wildest of the five, has died unexpectedly and the other four have come together for the first time in years. Suddenly each of these old friends has to wonder if the dark secret they've shared for so long is the reason for their troubles today . . . and if someone within the circle is trying to destroy them all.

"Lippman has long excelled at believable psychological suspense."
—The Guardian

"Laura Lippman's rich, multigenerational tale explores how relationships between friends, spouses, neighbors, parents, and children wound and sustain us." —O, The Oprah Magazine

ABOUT THE AUTHOR: **Laura Lippman** has been awarded every major prize in crime fiction. A recent recipient of the first Mayor's Prize, she lives in Baltimore, Maryland, and New Orleans with her husband, David Simon, stepson, and daughter.

May 2012 | Trade Paperback | Fiction | 368 pp | $14.99 | ISBN 9780062122926
William Morrow Paperbacks | harpercollins.com | lauralippman.com
Also available as: eBook

CONVERSATION STARTERS

1. The novel's epigraph is a poem by John Greenleaf Whittier and includes the lines ". . . pity us all, Who vainly the dreams of youth recall." Talk about the meaning of this line and how it relates to the story.

2. Go-Go is often referred to as bad. Was he a troubled child or just a handful? How did being around older children influence his behavior and who he was? Was his death a suicide? Why did he go back to drinking?

3. What role did Chicken George play in the five youths' lives? What was their fascination with him? How can a person be fascinated with— yet so incurious about—another person like Gwen and company were about Chicken George? How much of their lack of curiosity is their age and how much the kind of people they are?

4. "Clem believes every profession covers for its incompetents. So do families. Any group, no matter how loosely affiliated, will always close ranks against the world at large." Do you agree with Clem? What is the impact on individual lives and on society itself for all this covering up?

5. Why are parents so eager to protect their children from pain— whether it's getting emotionally hurt or having regrets? Isn't pain part of maturing? How do today's parents compare to the generation that came before? How and why have we changed?

6. If you were a child growing up in the seventies and eighties, how has life—and childhood itself—changed over the years? Do you agree with Clem that very few things about people have changed in his lifetime? Are our concerns and fears about our children real, or are much of our notions of the bad in the world products of a dark imagination fueled by the media?

7. Can Mickey, Go Go, Tim, Sean, and Gwen be excused for their actions because they were "only children"? At what age should a person know the difference between right and wrong?

8. Is it right that a parent is willing to kill for a child? Is vengeance a sign of manhood?

9. Why can some people forget the past so easily? Is there a price to be paid for burying the past? What power do secrets and guilt have in shaping our lives? After Go-Go's death, why couldn't Gwen leave the past go?

THE NIGHT CIRCUS
By Erin Morgenstern

The circus arrives without warning. No announcements precede it. It is simply there, when yesterday it was not. Within the black-and-white striped canvas tents is an utterly unique experience full of breathtaking amazements. It is called Le Cirque des Rêves, and it is only open at night.

But behind the scenes, a fierce competition is underway: a duel between two young magicians, Celia and Marco, who have been trained since childhood expressly for this purpose by their mercurial instructors. Unbeknownst to them both, this is a game in which only one can be left standing. Despite the high stakes, Celia and Marco soon tumble headfirst into love, setting off a domino effect of dangerous consequences, and leaving the lives of everyone, from the performers to the patrons, hanging in the balance.

"Get ready to be won over. . . . Part love story, part fable, and a knockout debut. . . . So sparklingly alive, you'll swear the pages are breathing in your hands. . . . The Night Circus defies both genres and expectations." —**The Boston Globe**

*"A riveting debut. The Night Circus pulls you into a world as dark as it is dazzling, fully-realized but still something out of a dream. You will not want to leave it." —***Téa Obreht, author of** *The Tiger's Wife*

ABOUT THE AUTHOR: **Erin Morgenstern** is a writer and a multimedia artist, who describes all her work as "fairy tales in one way or another." She lives in Massachusetts.

July 2012 | Trade Paperback | Fiction | 528 pp | $15.00 | ISBN 9780307744432
Anchor | randomhouse.com | erinmorgenstern.com
Also available as: eBook and Audiobook

CONVERSATION STARTERS

1. The novel frequently changes narrative perspective. How does this transition shape your reading of the novel and your connection to the characters and the circus? Why do you think the author chose to tell the story from varied perspectives?

2. What role does time play in the novel? From Friedrick Thiessen's clock to the delayed aging of the circus developers to the birth of the twins—is time manipulated or fated at the circus?

3. From the outside, the circus is full of enchantments and delights, but behind the scenes, the delicate push and pull of the competition results in some sinister events: i.e., Tara Burgess and Friedrick Thiessen's deaths. How much is the competition at fault for these losses and how much is it the individual's doing?

4. How do you view the morality of the circus in regards to the performers and developers being unknowing pawns in Celia and Marco's competition? Do Celia and Marco owe an explanation to their peers about their unwitting involvement?

5. Isobel is a silent, yet integral, partner in both the circus and the competition. She has an ally in Tsukiko, but seemingly no one else, especially not Marco. How much does Marco's underestimation of Isobel affect the outcome of the competition?

6. How does Isobel serve as a foil to Celia? Who, if anyone, fills that role for Marco?

7. Tsukiko is aware of Isobel's "tempering of the circus" from the outset and when Isobel worries that it is having no effect, Tsukiko suggests: "perhaps it is controlling the chaos within more than the chaos without." What, and whose, chaos is Tsukiko alluding to here?

8. Celia tells Bailey that he is "not destined or chosen" to be the next proprietor of the circus. He is simply "in the right place at the right time . . . and care[s] enough to do what needs to be done. Sometimes that's enough." In this situation, is that "enough?" Can the responsibility of maintaining the circus be trusted to just anyone, or unlike Celia suggests, is Bailey truly special?

9. At the closing of the novel, we are left to believe that the circus is still traveling—Bailey's business card provides an email address as his contact information. How do you think the circus would fare over time? Would the circus need to evolve to suit each generation or is it distinctive enough to transcend time?

NOTHING DAUNTED
The Unexpected Education of Two Society Girls in the West

By Dorothy Wickenden

In the summer of 1916, Dorothy Woodruff and Rosamond Underwood, bored by society luncheons, charity work, and the effete men who courted them, left their families in Auburn, New York, to teach school in the wilds of northwestern Colorado. They lived with a family of homesteaders in the Elkhead Mountains and rode to school on horseback, often in blinding blizzards. Their students walked or skied, in tattered clothes and shoes tied together with string. The young cattle rancher who had lured them west, Ferry Carpenter, had promised them the adventure of a lifetime. He hadn't let on that they would be considered dazzling prospective brides for the locals.

Nearly a hundred years later, Dorothy Wickenden, the granddaughter of Dorothy Woodruff, found the teachers' buoyant letters home, which captured the voices of the pioneer women, the children, and other unforgettable people the women got to know. In reconstructing their journey, Wickenden has created an exhilarating saga about two intrepid women and the "settling up" of the West.

"If you were impressed with Laura Hillenbrand's efforts to breathe life into Seabiscuit—*or wax romantic about Willa Cather's classic* My Antonia—*this is a book for you." —Grand Rapids Press*

ABOUT THE AUTHOR: **Dorothy Wickenden** has been the executive editor of *The New Yorker* since January 1996. She also writes for the magazine and is the moderator of its weekly podcast "The Political Scene." She is on the faculty of The Writers' Institute at CUNY's Graduate Center, where she teaches a course on narrative nonfiction. A former Nieman Fellow at Harvard, Wickenden was national affairs editor at *Newsweek* from 1993–1995 and before that was the longtime executive editor at *The New Republic*. She lives with her husband and her two daughters in Westchester, New York.

April 2012 | Trade Paperback | Fiction | 320 pp | $15.00 | ISBN 9781439176597
Scribner | simonandschuster.com | nothingdaunted.com
Also available as: eBook and Audiobook

CONVERSATION STARTERS

1. In the Prologue, Wickenden calls Ros's and Dorothy's adventure "an alternative Western." What do you think she means by this? After finishing the book, do you agree? How does their story compare to your idea of the classic "Western"?
2. How are Ros and Dorothy different from each other? How are they similar?
3. Each chapter opens with a photograph—from Dorothy teaching her students in 1917 in Chapter 10 to Bob Perry outside his cabin in Chapter 14. How did these pictures shape or enhance your reading of *Nothing Daunted*? How did they add to your understanding of the setting and time period?
4. Similarly, how did the inclusion of letters and notes enhance your reading? Was there one particular or memorable correspondence that stood out to you?
5. William H. Seward was known as a firebrand for representing the black defendant in a notorious murder case and for befriending abolitionist Harriet Tubman. What influence did Seward, Tubman, and other strong personalities in Auburn have on Dorothy and Ros?
6. How would you define Ros and Dorothy's teaching experience in one word? How did people react to their arrival in Elkhead? How did the girls' families react to their decision to leave the comforts of their homes in Auburn?
7. How would you describe Ferry Carpenter? Wickenden writes that he "believed that American democracy was born on the frontier." What effect did the lawlessness and opportunities of the West have on Ferry's imagination and aspirations? How did the frontier influence Ros and Dorothy?
8. After Ros and Dorothy applied to be teachers, Ferry was told that one of the applicants "was voted the best-looking girl in the junior class of Smith College!" What advantages—educational, social, physical—did Ros and Dorothy have over other applicants?
9. Ros and Dorothy received nearly identical scores on their Colorado teacher's exams. Ros wrote to her mother: "I think Mrs. Peck must have been perjuring her soul, to give [those scores] to us." What did she mean?
10. How did the structure of the narrative, with its flashbacks to the past and flash-forwards to the current day, influence how you read *Nothing Daunted*?

THE PARIS WIFE

By Paula McLain

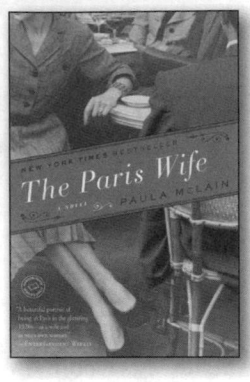

Chicago, 1920: Hadley Richardson is a quiet twenty-eight-year-old who has all but given up on love and happiness—until she meets Ernest Hemingway and her life changes forever. Following a whirlwind courtship and wedding, the pair set sail for Paris, where they become the golden couple in a lively and volatile group. Though deeply in love, the Hemingways are ill prepared for the hard-drinking and fast-living life of Jazz-Age Paris, which hardly values traditional notions of family and monogamy. Ernest struggles to find the voice that will earn him a place in history, pouring all the richness and intensity of his life with Hadley and their circle of friends into the novel that will become *The Sun Also Rises*. Hadley, meanwhile, strives to hold on to her sense of self as the demands of life with Ernest grow costly and her roles as wife, friend, and muse become more challenging. Despite their extraordinary bond, they eventually find themselves facing the ultimate crisis of their marriage.

A heartbreaking portrayal of love and torn loyalty, *The Paris Wife* is all the more poignant because we know that, in the end, Hemingway wrote that he would rather have died than fallen in love with anyone but Hadley.

"McLain smartly explores Hadley's ambivalence about her role as supportive wife to a budding genius. . . . Women and book groups are going to eat up this novel." —USA Today

About the Author: **Paula McLain** was born in Fresno, California, in 1965. She received her MFA in poetry from the University of Michigan in 1996, and since then has been a resident at Yaddo and the recipient of fellowships from the National Endowment for the Arts. She is the author of two collections of poetry, a much-praised memoir, and one previous and well-received novel, *A Ticket to Ride*. Paula McLain lives in Cleveland, Ohio, with her family.

November 2012 | Trade Paperback | Fiction | 352 pp | $14.00 | ISBN 9780345521316
Ballantine Books | randomhouse.com
Also available as: eBook and Audiobook

CONVERSATION STARTERS

1. Hadley and Ernest don't get a lot of encouragement from their friends and family when they decided to marry. What seems to draw the two together? What are some of the strengths of their initial attraction and partnership?

2. Throughout *The Paris Wife*, Hadley refers to herself as "Victorian" as opposed to "modern." What are some of the ways she doesn't feel like she fits into life in bohemian Paris? How does this impact her relationship with Ernest? Her self-esteem?

3. Hadley and Ernest's marriage survived for many years in Jazz-Age Paris, an environment that had very little patience for monogamy and other traditional values. What in their relationship seems to sustain them?

4. One of the most wrenching scenes in the book is when Hadley loses a valise containing all of Ernest's work to date. What kind of turning point does this mark for the Hemingway's marriage? Do you think Ernest ever forgives her?

5. In *The Paris Wife*, when Ernest receives his contract for *In Our Time*, Hadley says, "He would never again be unknown. We would never again be this happy." How did fame affect Ernest and his relationship with Hadley?

6. *The Sun Also Rises* is drawn from the Hemingways' real-life experiences with bullfighting in Spain. Ernest and his friends are clearly present in the book, but Hadley is not. Why? In what ways do you think Hadley is instrumental to the book regardless?

7. What was the nature of the relationship between Hadley and Pauline Pfeiffer? Were they legitimately friends? How do you see Pauline taking advantage of her intimate position in the Hemingway's life? Do you think Hadley is naïve for not suspecting Pauline of having designs on Ernest earlier? Why or why not?

8. What would it have cost for Hadley to stick it out with Ernest no matter what? Is there a way she could have fought harder for her marriage?

9. When Hemingway's biographer Carlos Baker interviewed Hadley Richardson near the end of her life, he expected her to be bitter, and yet she persisted in describing Ernest as a "prince." How can she have continued to love and admire him after the way he hurt her?

10. Ernest Hemingway spent the last months of his life tenderly reliving his first marriage in the pages his memoir, *A Moveable Feast*. In fact, it was the last thing he wrote before his death. Do you think he realized what he'd truly lost with Hadley?

PICTURE THIS

By Jacqueline Sheehan

The poignant and unforgettable sequel to the beloved bestseller *Lost & Found*; a marvelous tale of life-altering surprises and unanticipated guests.

Peaks Island, Maine, vibrates with its own special magic, a unique flow to life that knits together the small community that calls it home. The people, the animals, and even the houses have a charm and personality all their own. Just ask Rocky Pelligrino. Devastated by her husband Bob's sudden death, she found hope thanks to a relentlessly loyal black Lab named Cooper. Warm friends and a new job— as the island's animal control warden—have helped Rocky chart a course toward a promising future. She's even ready to try love again with Hill, the gentle and patient archery instructor. And there is an old house haunted by lost love and forgotten secrets that speaks to her soul.

But a phone call from a troubled young woman looking for her biological father shakes Rocky's newfound joy. Could this young girl hold a tendril of the man who was the love of her life? Or could the girl's appearance throw Rocky's world into chaos . . . and shatter her heart again?

"Sheehan uses her skills as both a psychologist and a writer to create a solid, insightful story that will leave fans eagerly awaiting another visit from the strong heroine, her dog and her friends." —Kirkus Reviews

ABOUT THE AUTHOR: **Jacqueline Sheehan, Ph.D.**, is a fiction writer and essayist, the bestselling author of the novels *Lost & Found* and *Now & Then*. Currently on the faculty of Writers in Progress and Grub Street in Massachusetts, she also offers international workshops on the combination of yoga and writing. She writes travel articles about lesser-known destinations and lives in Massachusetts.

June 2012 | Trade Paperback | Fiction | 400 pp | $14.99 | ISBN 9780062008121
William Morrow Paperbacks | harpercollins.com | jacquelinesheehan.com
Also available as: eBook

CONVERSATION STARTERS

1. Rocky is caught between wanting to start a new relationship with Hill and grieving the sudden death of her husband. Does it seem unimaginable to fall in love again after the death of a spouse, or would it feel like a second chance?

2. Rocky is instantly drawn to Natalie in a way that seems to defy her psychological knowledge. What is it that pulls Rocky to the wayward girl?

3. How does Natalie's background influence her behaviors with Rocky and with others on Peaks Island?

4. The house that Rocky buys is brimming with personality. The house makes a wish when Rocky first stands in front of it. "Give me one more go at it." How does Rocky's decision at the end of the book answer this wish?

5. How does Cooper respond to Natalie? If not for Melissa's photo, would anyone be able to detect his hesitation with Natalie? How is the micro detection of the camera like Cooper's perception of the world? What can the camera see that the naked eye cannot?

6. Tess and her granddaughter Danielle are extremely close. Aside from sharing synesthesia (even though Tess loses hers after surgery), how else are their sensibilities similar?

7. Natalie picks Danielle, the most tender spirit on the island, to include in her plan of revenge. Are there any other reasons why Natalie picks the child?

8. Melissa is immediately suspicious of Natalie. How can teenagers see each other so clearly?

9. In this story, who are the Tzadikum nistarim?

THE PROMISE OF STARDUST
By Priscille Sibley

Matt Beaulieu and Elle McClure share a lifelong love, but after an accident leaves her with severe brain damage and no hope of recovery, he agrees to take her off life support until he finds out that she is pregnant. Not everyone believes it is possible to save the baby Elle's carrying, and some believe it is morally wrong to keep her on the ventilator because she had an advanced health care directive that stated that she would never want extraordinary measures taken to extend her life. Matt still wants to try.

"In this brave novel, a family making choices about death with dignity finds themselves in uncomfortable opposition . . . explores with compassion and insight, how political and personal needs align and shift." —**Randy Susan Meyers, author of** *The Murderer's Daughters*

About the Author: **Priscille Sibley** is a neonatal intensive care nurse who lives in New Jersey with her husband and three teenage sons. Her short fiction has appeared in *MiPOesias* and her poetry in *The Shine Journal*. She is a member of Backspace Writer's Forum and Liberty State Fiction Writers. *The Promise of Stardust* is her first novel.

February 2013 | Trade Paperback | Fiction | 416 pp | $15.99 | ISBN 978006219176
William Morrow Paperbacks | harpercollins.com | priscillesibley.com
Also available as: eBook

CONVERSATION STARTERS

1. As a neurosurgeon, Matt immediately realizes that Elle's brain damage is severe. Why do you think he lets Phil operate? Do you think he betrays Elle by letting Phil do so? What about when Matt decides to keep his wife on life support?
2. Do you think Linney is overstepping her bounds when she opposes Matt's decision to keep Elle on life support?
3. As teenagers, Matt and Elle find themselves about to have a baby. What do you think would have happened if Matt had approached his parents for help?
4. When Elle miscarries the first time, she says a name is important because it is the only thing they will ever be able to give the baby. Do you think it's important to give a name to grief?
5. Matt wants to keep the court case private, but it becomes a media circus. How much influence does the media have on events like this? How much should they have? Is their involvement an expression of freedom of speech or is it an invasion of privacy?
6. Matt keeps talking to Elle while she's in the hospital, even though he knows she can't hear him. Why do you think he does that?
7. Elle says women are stronger because they can discuss their sadness and men feel as though they have to mask their pain and insecurities. Do you think that's true?
8. Do you think Elle or Linney actually hastened Alice's death? Do you think Matt would have actually gone to the authorities with Elle's diary? Would you have given Alice an extra "dose" to relieve her suffering?
9. Matt tried desperately to resuscitate his and Elle's stillborn son. How do you think that loss affected Matt? Elle? And, as a doctor, was Matt's "failure" to save the baby a deeper loss for him?
10. Why do you think Elle never gave Matt her medical power of attorney? Have you made an advance directive? Who would you designate to make those decisions for you?
11. At the end of the story, Matt sees a fleeting figure in the trees and for a moment he thinks it is Elle. In the aftermath of loss have you ever briefly forgotten that your loved one is gone? Do you believe some part of them stays with you forever?
12. In some states, pregnancy invalidates a woman's advanced directive. Are you familiar with the laws in your state? Would you want to be kept on life support if you were pregnant?

QUIET
The Power of Introverts in a World That Can't Stop Talking

By Susan Cain

At least one-third of the people we know are introverts. They are the ones who prefer listening to speaking, reading to partying; who innovate and create but dislike self-promotion; who favor working on their own over brainstorming in teams. Although they are often labeled "quiet," it is to introverts that we owe many of the great contributions to society—from van Gogh's sunflowers to the invention of the personal computer.

Passionately argued, impressively researched, and filled with indelible stories of real people, *Quiet* shows how dramatically we undervalue introverts, and how much we lose in doing so. This extraordinary book has the power to permanently change how we see introverts and, equally important, how introverts see themselves.

"Superbly researched, deeply insightful, and a fascinating read, Quiet *is an indispensable resource for anyone who wants to understand the gifts of the introverted half of the population."* —**Gretchen Rubin, author of** *The Happiness Project*

"A startling, important, and readable page-turner that will make quiet people see themselves in a whole new light." —**Naomi Wolf, author of** *The Beauty Myth*

About the Author: **Susan Cain** is the author of *The New York Times* bestseller *Quiet: The Power of Introverts in A World That Can't Stop Talking*, which is being translated into thirty languages. Her writing has appeared in *The New York Times*; *The Atlantic*; the *Dallas Morning News*; O, *The Oprah Magazine*; Time.com; and PsychologyToday.com. She lives in the Hudson River Valley with her husband and two sons.

January 2012 | Hardcover | Nonfiction | 352 pp | $26.00 | ISBN 9780307352149
Paperback available January 2013 (ISBN 9780307352156; $16.00)
Crown | randomhouse.com | thepowerofintroverts.com
Also available as: eBook and Audiobook
To inquire about having the author visit your reading group via phone or video chat, please email crownreadinggroups@randomhouse.com

....

CONVERSATION STARTERS

1. Based on the quiz in the book, do you think you're an introvert, an extrovert, or an ambivert? Are you an introvert in some situations and an extrovert in others?
2. What about the important people in your lives—your partner, your friends, your kids?
3. Which parts of *Quiet* resonated most strongly with you? Were there parts you disagreed with—and if so, why?
4. Can you think of a time in your life when being an introvert proved to be an advantage?
5. Who are your favorite introverted role models?
6. Do you agree with the author that introverts can be good leaders? What role do you think charisma plays in leadership? Can introverts be charismatic?
7. If you're an introvert, what do you find most challenging about working with extroverts?
8. If you're an extrovert, what do you find most challenging about working with introverts?
9. *Quiet* explains how Western society evolved from a Culture of Character to a Culture of Personality. Are there enclaves in our society where a Culture of Character still holds sway? What would a twenty-first-century Culture of Character look like?
10. *Quiet* talks about the New Groupthink, the value system holding that creativity and productivity emerge from group work rather than individual thought. Have you experienced this in your own workplace?
11. Do you think your job suits your temperament? If not, what could you do to change things?
12. If you have children, how does your temperament compare to theirs? How do you handle areas in which you're not temperamentally compatible?
13. If you're in a relationship, how does your temperament compare to that of your partner? How do you handle areas in which you're not compatible?
14. Do you enjoy social media such as Facebook and Twitter, and do you think this has something to do with your temperament?
15. *Quiet* talks about "restorative niches," the places introverts go or the things they do to recharge their batteries. What are your favorite restorative niches?
16. Susan Cain calls for a Quiet Revolution. Would you like to see this kind of a movement take place, and if so, what is the number-one change you'd like to see happen?

THE RED BOOK
By Deborah Copaken Kogan

Clover, Addison, Mia, and Jane were roommates at Harvard until their graduation in 1989. Clover, homeschooled on a commune by mixed-race parents, felt woefully out of place. Addison yearned to shed the burden of her Mayflower heritage. Mia mined the depths of her suburban ennui to enact brilliant performances on the Harvard stage. Jane, an adopted Vietnamese war orphan, made sense of her fractured world through words. Twenty years later, their lives are in free fall. Clover, once a securities broker with Lehman, is out of a job and struggling to reproduce before her fertility window slams shut. Addison's marriage to a writer's-blocked novelist is as stale as her so-called career as a painter. Hollywood shut its gold-plated gates to Mia, who now stays home with her four children, renovating and acquiring faster than her director husband can pay the bills. Jane, the Paris bureau chief for a newspaper whose foreign bureaus are now shuttered, is caught in a vortex of loss.

Like all Harvard grads, they've kept abreast of one another via the red book, a class report published every five years, containing brief autobiographical essays by fellow alumni. But there's the story we tell the world, and then there's the real story, as these former classmates will learn during their twentieth reunion weekend.

"The Red Book, *which is filled with Deborah Copaken Kogan's smart take on everything from friendship to sex to child raising to getting over the past— or not—makes for old-school compulsive reading.*" —**Meg Wolitzer, author of** The Uncoupling

ABOUT THE AUTHOR: **Deborah Copaken Kogan** is the author of *Between Here and April*, a novel, and *Shutterbabe*, her bestselling memoir about her years as a war photographer. She lives in Harlem, New York, with her husband and three children.

April 2012 | Hardcover | Fiction | 368 pp | $24.99 | ISBN 9781401340827
Available in paperback May 2013
Voice | hyperionbooks.com | deborahcopakenkogan.com
Also available as: eBook

CONVERSATION STARTERS

1. *The Red Book* is peopled with a broad range of characters. Discuss how successfully you feel the author wrote from the point of view of individuals of so many different social and financial backgrounds, sexual orientations, ethnic identifications, and religious beliefs.
2. Both Addison and Mia studied creative arts in college but stopped pursuing their respective fields professionally once they were married and began having kids. Do you feel their stories ring particularly true? Would it have been possible for either one to have led a balanced life while pursuing her passion, and if so, which one(s) and why?
3. Consider the different biases and aversions these characters have. What kind of comment does *The Red Book* make about our worst fears, prejudices, and biases and the ways we let them govern our lives?
4. While sex is not the only culprit behind the marital discord in these romantic relationships, it plays a large role in the dynamics of its characters' lives. Consider the way this novel portrays the importance of sex in a long-term relationship, and discuss whether or not the lessons learned by these characters ring particularly true.
5. *The Red Book* also highlights our human tendency to compare ourselves with peers and to judge the ways and means by which we have lived our lives. The characters in the novel do this every five years via Harvard's red book, and also through social Web sites like Facebook. What comment is Kogan making about our compulsion to compare ourselves with others?
6. This novel also explores, to some extent, mother-daughter relationships. Discuss the ways in which Jane's discovery of her mother's infidelity challenges Jane's perception of her mother and marriage in general; the ways in which the sections narrated from Trilby's point of view avoid typical depictions of teenage rebellion; and the ways in which Mia's life is both a mirror and a foil to that of her mother's. What does each relationship reveal about the power, influence, and pitfalls of the mother-daughter connection?
7. How does the close friendship of Mia, Clover, Addison, and Jane resemble your own close friendships from college and/or high school? What are the redeeming aspects of each character, and what makes them worth following throughout the novel, despite their faults? What part of their friendship is enviable? Is there any part of their friendship that you found unusual, or maybe even unenviable?

REMEMBERING THE MUSIC, FORGETTING THE WORDS

Travels With Mom in the Land of Dementia

By Kate Whouley

Winner of the New England Book Award in Non Fiction

Kate Whouley is a smart, single woman who faces life head-on. Her mother, Anne, is a strong-minded accidental feminist with a weakness for unreliable men. Their complicated relationship isn't simplified when Anne exhibits symptoms of organic memory loss. As Kate becomes her mother's advocate and protector, Kate will discover that the demon we call Alzheimer's is also an unlikely teacher—and healer. A contemporary mother-daughter story with universal appeal, *Remembering the Music, Forgetting the Words*, is written with the same "good humor and thoughtful humanity" that Anna Quindlen admired in the author's first memoir, *Cottage for Sale, Must Be Moved*, a perennial reading group favorite. Named to the American Library Association's Best of the Best list for 2012, *Remembering the Music*, in the words of novelist David Payne "concerns the most important issues: family, mortality, our aloneness in the world, our connection in the face of it."

"...often humorous and always compassionate....Whouley is a smooth operator." —**Janice Lloyd, USA TODAY**

"Contemporary subject matter and wide appeal make this is an outstanding choice for public libraries—highly recommended for book clubs." —**Barbara Morrow Williams, American Library Association Citation**

About the Author: **Kate Whouley** lives and writes on Cape Cod. An avocational flutist, she also volunteers for the Cape & Islands Art and Alzheimer's initiative. *Remembering the Music* is an Indie Next Pick and a winner of the New England Book Award. Kate Whouley's first book, *Cottage for Sale, Must Be Moved*, was a Book Sense Book-of-the-Year nominee.

September 2012 | Trade Paperback | Memoir | 240 pp | $16.00 | ISBN 9780807003312
Beacon Press | beacon.org | katewhouley.com
Also available as an eBook. Audiobook available from Audible.com

CONVERSATION STARTERS

1. In the opening chapter, we learn that Kate Whouley's mother Anne is a strong, intelligent woman and a role model for her daughter. In Chapter Six we learn their relationship is more complicated. Did your expectations for their journey change as you learned more about their past? How are family relationships complicated or enhanced by shared history?

2. In the absence of siblings or a partner, Kate finds support in friends, particularly her longtime girlfriends. Do you have friends who feel like family, or family members who feel like friends? How do you balance friendship and family?

3. Kate also seeks support and assistance from Suzanne, a professional in elder care. How does Suzanne help Kate to see her mother differently? Can you think of a situation in your family or personal life in which an outsider helped you gain perspective? How or why?

4. Kate, in Chapter Thirteen, mentions she has never thought of her relationship with her mother as particularly "close." Would you agree with her characterization? How does their relationship change during the course of the book?

5. How does Kate's understanding of Alzheimer's disease evolve over time? Does her increasing awareness affect her attitudes toward others in her life?

6. Kate makes a connection between playing music and caring for a person with Alzheimer's. What is it? How might this approach be relevant to non-musicians? Can you think of other activities that require a similar sense of being present?

7. On page 105, Kate writes: "Our elders move from strength to debility and debility becomes the norm." Have you ever had to make accommodations for aging elders in your life? In what ways was your experience similar to Kate's? In what ways was your experience different?

8. "Memory is overrated," the author declares on page 186. What does she believe is more important? Do you agree or disagree?

9. In Chapter Twenty-Four, Kate describes a series of dreams she has after Anne's death. How would you interpret the final dream in that series? Why do you think the author chose to share her dreams with readers?

10. The author ends the book with a description of a concert performance. How does this narrative choice affirm Kate's enduring connection to her mother? Can you think of more than one way to interpret the title, *Remembering the Music*?

THE REPORT

By Jessica Frances Kane

A stunning first novel and a vivid exploration of the way tragedies are reported, remembered, and commemorated, based on a real-life WWII tragedy

On a March night in 1943, on the steps of a London tube station, 173 people die in a crowd seeking shelter from another air raid. When the devastated neighborhood demands a report, the job falls to magistrate Laurence Dunne. As Dunne investigates, he finds the truth to be precarious, even damaging. He struggles to complete his task without causing hurt. Yet when he is forced to reflect several decades later, Dunne must consider whether he chose the right course. *The Report* is a compelling commentary on the way all tragedies are remembered.

"Nothing less than perfect." —**Newsday**

"A page-turner." —**National Public Radio**

"Compelling." —**More Magazine**

"It blew me away." —**Boston Phoenix**

"Stunning." —**Star Tribune**

"Marvelous." —**Kirkus Reviews**

"I was absolutely riveted." —**Anthony Doerr, author of *The Shell Collector***

About the Author: **Jessica Francis Kane** is the author of the story collection *Bending Heaven*. Her stories have been broadcast on BBC radio and have appeared in a many publications, including *Virginia Quarterly Review*, *McSweeney's*, the *Missouri Review*, and *Michigan Quarterly Review*. Her essays and humor pieces have appeared in *McSweeney's Internet Tendency* and the *Morning News*, where she is a contributing writer. She lives in New York with her husband and their daughter and son.

September 2012 | Trade Paperback | Fiction | 256 pp | $15.00 | ISBN 9781555975654
Graywolf Press | graywolfpress.org | jessicafranciskane.com
Also available as: eBook

CONVERSATION STARTERS

1. Throughout *The Report*, Jessica Francis Kane does a wonderful job of dropping hints regarding what really happened on the night of March 3. Did you notice these hints as you read? If so, did they help you to figure out Ada's role in the matter before Laurie revealed it?

2. The novel is structured so that the narrative moves back and forth between 1943 and 1973. How did this enhance your reading? Did you find it effective and satisfying when the two stories synced up at the novel's end?

3. At the beginning of the third section, Kane writes: "The tragedy does not remain the story. As with any other public property, it is transformed by use." Do you agree with this statement? What contemporary tragedies do you think have been "transformed by use"?

4. Several chapters in the novel's third section consist of snippets of conversations between Laurie and the witnesses. Did you find these anonymous accounts compelling? What kind of effect do you think Kane was after?

5. During questioning, Constable Henderson says to Laurie, "It's hard, sir, to know what's right." Do you believe that sometimes accidents are unavoidable? Do you think the crush could have been prevented?

6. During his conversation with Reverend McNeely after writing the report, Laurie says that "perhaps we should only sometimes be held accountable for the unintended consequences of our actions." Do you think Ada Barber is responsible for the deadly crush? Or do you agree with Laurie that she shouldn't be held accountable?

7. After James Low's funeral, Ada comes to this conclusion: "Surviving some disasters . . . you don't get to be happy again. You simply change, and then you decide if you can live with the change." Do you agree with this or do you think that tragedy can transform some people for the better? Is it ever really possible to move on from a tragedy?

8. The novel's last chapter seems to be the actual report Laurie wrote yet reads as something more lyrical and poetic. Do you think this is just a meditative final chapter? Or do you think this was the report Laurie originally submitted? Do you think it is an accurate reporting of the incident?

9. What sort of similarities, if any, do you see between the cultural impact of the report and the 9/11 Commission Report?

RULES OF CIVILITY
By Amor Towles

Set in New York City in 1938, *Rules of Civility* tells the story of a watershed year in the life of an uncompromising twenty-five-year-old named Katey Kontent. Katey embarks on a journey from a Wall Street secretarial pool through the upper echelons of New York society in search of a brighter future.

The story opens on New Year's Eve in a Greenwich Village jazz bar, where Katey and her roommate Eve happen to meet Tinker Grey, a handsome banker. This chance encounter and its startling consequences cast Katey off her current course, but ends up providing her unexpected access to the rarified offices of Conde Nast and a glittering new social circle. Befriended in turn by a shy, principled multimillionaire, an Upper East Side ne'er-do-well, and a single-minded widow who is ahead of her times, Katey has the chance to experience firsthand the poise secured by wealth and station, but also the aspirations, envy, disloyalty, and desires that reside just below the surface. Even as she waits for circumstances to bring Tinker back into her orbit, she will learn how individual choices become the means by which life crystallizes loss.

"The new novel we couldn't put down . . . in the crisp, noirish prose of the era, Towles portrays complex relationships in a city that is at once melting pot and elitist enclave—and a thoroughly modern heroine who fearlessly claims her place in it." —O, the Oprah Magazine

ABOUT THE AUTHOR: **Amor Towles** was raised in a suburb of Boston, Massachusetts. He graduated from Yale College and received an M.A. in English from Stanford University where he was a Scowcroft Fellow. He is a principal at an investment firm in Manhattan, where he lives with his wife and two children. He is on the boards of the Library of America and the Yale Art Gallery.

June 2012 | Trade Paperback | Fiction | 352 pp | $16.00 | ISBN 9780143121169
Penguin Books | us.penguingroup.com | amortowles.com
Also available as: eBook and Audiobook

CONVERSATION STARTERS

1. At the outset, *Rules of Civility* appears to be about the interrelationship between Katey, Tinker, and Eve; but then events quickly lead Eve and Tinker off stage. Are Dicky Vanderwhile, Wallace Wolcott, Bitsy, Peaches, Hank and Anne Grandyn as essential to Katey's "story" as Tinker and Eve?

2. Katey observes at one point that Agatha Christie "doles out her little surprises at the carefully calibrated pace of a nanny dispensing sweets to the children in her care." Something similar could be said of how Katey doles out information about herself. What sort of things is Katey slow to reveal?

3. After seeing Tinker at Chinoisserie, Katey indicts George Washington's *Rules of Civility* as "A do-it-yourself charm school. A sort of How to Win Friends and Influence People 150 years ahead of its time." But Dicky sees some nobility in Tinker's aspiration to Washington's rules. Where does your judgment fall on Tinker? Is Katey wholly innocent of Tinker's crime? Where does simulation end and character begin? Which of Washington's rules do you aspire to?

4. A central theme in the book is that a chance encounter or cursory decision in one's twenties can shape one's course for decades to come. Do you think this is true to life? Were there casual encounters or decisions that you made, which in retrospect were watershed events?

5. When Eve says, "I like it just fine on this side of the windshield" what does she mean? And why is the life Tinker offers her so contrary to the new life she intends to pursue?

6. When Tinker sets out on his new life, why does he intend to start his days saying Katey's name? What does he mean when he describes Katey as someone of "such poise and purpose"?

7. T.S. Eliot's *The Love Song of J. Alfred Prufrock*" is referenced in the book's Preface and its Epilogue. Why is that poem somehow central to Katey's 1969 reflections on her 1938 experiences?

8. In the Epilogue, Katey observes that "Right choices are the means by which life crystallizes loss." What is a right choice that you have made and what did you leave behind as a result?

THE SECRETS OF MARY BOWSER
By Lois Leveen

Based on a remarkable true story, *The Secrets of Mary Bowser* is an inspiring tale of one daring woman's willingness to sacrifice her own freedom to change the course of history.

All her life, Mary has been a slave to the wealthy Van Lew family of Richmond, Virginia. But when Bet, the willful Van Lew daughter, decides to send Mary to Philadelphia to be educated, she must leave her family to seize her freedom.

Life in the North brings new friendships, a courtship, and a far different education than Mary ever expected, one that leads her into the heart of the abolition movement. With the nation edging toward war, she defies Virginia law by returning to Richmond to care for her ailing father—and to fight for emancipation. Posing as a slave in the Confederate White House in order to spy on President Jefferson Davis, Mary deceives even those who are closest to her to aid the Union command.

Just when it seems that all her courageous gambles to end slavery will pay off, Mary discovers that everything comes at a cost—even freedom.

"Deftly balancing history, romance and adventure, Leveen honors the life and historical importance of a brave, resourceful woman." —**Kirkus Reviews**

"Masterfully written, The Secrets of Mary Bowser *shines a new light onto our country's darkest history. Balancing fire and grace, the story of Mary Bowser is an ethical journey we won't soon forget, one that takes us from hatred to courage to love."* —**Brunonia Barry, bestselling author of *The Lace Reader* and *The Map of True Places***

ABOUT THE AUTHOR: Award-winning author **Lois Leveen's** work has appeared in the *New York Times*, on NPR, and in literary journals and anthologies. A former faculty member at UCLA and Reed College, she lives in Portland, Oregon.

May 2012 | Trade Paperback | Fiction | 496 pp | $15.99 | ISBN 9780062107909
William Morrow Paperbacks | harpercollins.com | loisleveen.com
Also available as: eBook

CONVERSATION STARTERS

1. Often when we think of slavery, we think of plantations. How does slavery in Richmond differ from plantation slavery? How is it similar? What did you find most surprising about the lives of slaves and of free blacks in Richmond?

2. Though both of Mary's parents were born in slavery, their experiences of slavery were quite different: her mother was raised in New York, was taught to read, and worked as a house slave; her father was born on a plantation and performed skilled labor at the smithy. How do these differences shape the characters?

3. When Bet frees her slaves, Mary and her parents face a difficult choice because of Virginia law. Was Bet being selfish and headstrong when she chose to emancipate the Van Lew slaves without considering how being forced out of the community would affect them? Or was she doing the right thing by letting Mary's family and the other freed slaves decide on their own what to do?

4. When we read the novel, we already know that during the war Lincoln signs the Emancipation Proclamation, and that after the Union victory, all the slaves become free. But Mary chooses to walk back into slavery without knowing for sure that these things will happen. How does living free in Philadelphia shape her willingness to return to slavery in Richmond?

5. Mary's mother is certain that Jesus has a plan for her daughter. At times, Mary seems to share this belief, but at other times she doubts it. Wilson says her spying is the right thing to do, regardless. Do you think it matters whether Mary is choosing for herself to be a spy or whether she is fulfilling a plan that someone else has for her?

6. Theodore and Wilson are very different. What attracts Mary to each of them? Do you see ways that her experience of being courted by Theodore affects her relationship with Wilson?

7. Over the course of the novel, Mary learns to trust a series of white people: Zinnie Moore, Thomas McNiven, Bet Van Lew, and Bet's mother. What are the qualities that Mary finds easiest to trust in each, and what are the things that challenge her trust?

8. The American playwright Eugene O'Neill wrote, "The past is the present, isn't it? It's the future, too." What does America today share with the past depicted in the novel?

THE SENSE OF AN ENDING

By Julian Barnes

A novel so compelling that it begs to be read in a single setting, *The Sense of an Ending* has the psychological and emotional depth and sophistication of Henry James at his best, and is a stunning new chapter in Julian Barnes's oeuvre.

This intense novel follows Tony Webster, a middle-aged man, as he contends with a past he never thought much about—until his closest childhood friends return with a vengeance: one of them from the grave, another maddeningly present. Tony thought he left this all behind as he built a life for himself, and his career has provided him with a secure retirement and an amicable relationship with his ex-wife and daughter, who now has a family of her own. But when he is presented with a mysterious legacy, he is forced to revise his estimation of his own nature and place in the world.

"Dense with philosophical ideas. . . . It manages to create genuine suspense as a sort of psychological detective story." —**Michiko Kakutani, *The New York Times***

"A page-turner, and when you finish you will return immediately to the beginning." —San Francisco Chronicle

ABOUT THE AUTHOR: **Julian Barnes** is the author of ten previous novels, three books of short stories, and three collections of journalism. In addition to the Booker Prize, his other honors include the Somerset Maugham Award, the Geoffrey Faber Memorial Prize, and the E.M. Forster Award from the American Academy of Arts and Letters. He lives in London.

May 2012 | Trade Paperback | Fiction | 176 pp | $14.95 | ISBN 9780307947727
Vintage | randomhouse.com | julianbarnes.com
Also available as: eBook

CONVERSATION STARTERS

1. What does the title mean?
2. The novel opens with a handful of water-related images. What is the significance of each? How does Barnes use water as a metaphor?
3. The phrase "Eros and Thanatos," or sex and death, comes up repeatedly in the novel. What did you take it to mean?
4. At school, Adrian says, "we need to know the history of the historian in order to understand the version that is being put in front of us." How does this apply to Tony's narration?
5. Did Tony love Veronica? How did his weekend with her family change their relationship?
6. When Mrs. Ford told Tony, "Don't let Veronica get away with too much," what did she mean? Why was this one sentence so important?
7. Veronica accuses Tony of being cowardly, while Tony considers himself peaceable. Whose assessment is more accurate?
8. What is the metaphor of the Severn Bore? Why does Tony's recollection of Veronica's presence change?
9. In addition to Adrian's earlier statement about history, Barnes offers other theories: Adrian also says, "History is that certainty produced at the point where the imperfections of memory meet the inadequacies of documentation," and Tony says, "History isn't the lies of the victors . . . It's more the memories of the survivors, most of whom are neither victorious nor defeated." Which of these competing notions do you think is most accurate? Which did Tony come to believe?
10. Discuss the character Margaret. What role does she play in Tony's story?
11. Why does Mrs. Ford make her bequest to Tony, after so many years? And why does Veronica characterize the £500 as "blood money"?
12. After rereading the letter he sent to Adrian and Veronica, Tony claims to feel remorse. Do you believe him? What do his subsequent actions tell us?
13. When Veronica refuses to turn over the diary to Tony, why doesn't he give up? Why does he continue to needle her for it?
14. What is Tony's opinion of himself? Of Adrian? How do both opinions change by the end of the novel?
15. How does the revelation in the final pages change your understanding of Veronica's actions?
16. Discuss the closing lines of the novel: "There is accumulation. There is responsibility. And beyond these, there is unrest. There is great unrest."

SHARP OBJECTS
By Gillian Flynn

Words are like a road map to reporter Camille Preaker's troubled past. Fresh from a brief stay at a psych hospital, Camille's first assignment from the second-rate daily paper where she works brings her reluctantly back to her hometown to cover the murders of two preteen girls.

Since she left town eight years ago, Camille has hardly spoken to her neurotic, hypochondriac mother or to the half-sister she barely knows: a beautiful thirteen-year-old with an eerie grip on the town. Now, installed again in her family's Victorian mansion, Camille is haunted by the childhood tragedy she has spent her whole life trying to cut from her memory.

As Camille works to uncover the truth about these violent crimes, she finds herself identifying with the young victims—a bit too strongly. Clues keep leading to dead ends, forcing Camille to unravel the psychological puzzle of her own past to get at the story. Dogged by her own demons, Camille will have to confront what happened to her years before if she wants to survive this homecoming.

*"To say this is a terrific debut is really too mild . . . I found myself dreading the last thirty pages or so but was helpless to stop turning there. Then, after the lights were out, the sting just stayed there in my head, coiling and hissing, like a snake in a cave." —***Stephen King**

About the Author: **Gillian Flynn** is the author of *The New York Times* bestseller *Dark Places*, which was a *New Yorker* Reviewers' Favorite, *Weekend* TODAY Top Summer Read, *Publishers Weekly* Best Book of 2009, and *Chicago Tribune* Favorite Fiction choice; and the Dagger Award winner *Sharp Objects*, which was an Edgar nominee for Best First novel, a BookSense pick, and a Barnes & Noble Discover selection. Her work has been published in twenty-eight countries. She lives in Chicago with her husband and son.

July 2007 | Trade Paperback | Fiction | 272 pp | $14.00 | ISBN 9780307341556
Broadway | randomhouse.com | gillian-flynn.com
Also available as: eBook and Audiobook
Gillian Flynn's other **Reading Group Choices'** selections: *Gone Girl* and *Dark Places*

CONVERSATION STARTERS

1. Soon after arriving in Wind Gap, Camille reflects, "Curry was wrong: Being an insider was more distracting than useful." What exactly was Curry wrong about? What advantages did he think Camille's "insider" status would bring with it? Was he, ultimately, wrong?

2. After ten years of abstinence, what is it that motivates Camille's promiscuity during her return to Wind Gap? What do you make of her choice of partners—both relative outsiders in the town?

3. Does Amma feel real affection for Camille? What are her motivations for getting closer to Camille?

4. Camille is addicted to "cutting," a form of self-harm. Why do you think she specifically cuts words into her skin?

5. Camille is shocked when her suspicions about Marian's illnesses are confirmed. Do you think she believes Adora deliberately killed Marian? Do you believe Marian's death was intentional?

6. How would you describe Alan—a man who, as Camille says, never sweats—living among so much anxiety? Do you see this type of contrast—between cleanliness and filth, order and disorder—elsewhere in the book?

7. Discuss the role of substance abuse in the book. How does it define the characters, their behavior, and the town of Wind Gap? How does it contribute to the telling of the story, as the focus—and the substances themselves—intensify during the course of the book?

8. Discuss the theme of violence throughout the book, including animal slaughter, sexual assault, cutting, biting, and, of course, murder. What do you make of the way residents of Wind Gap respond to violence?

9. Why does Camille allow herself to be poisoned by Adora?

10. In describing her crimes, Amma recalls happy, "wild" times with Ann and Natalie. Why isn't Amma able to keep these girls as friends? Do their violent undercurrents doom these friendships to fail, or could they have been overcome?

11. At the end of the book, Camille isn't certain of her answer to one key question: "Was I good at caring for Amma because of kindness? Or did I like caring for Amma because I have Adora's sickness?" What is your opinion?

12. How important do you think the outward appearance of the people in *Sharp Objects* is to their personalities? Ugliness and beauty are themes throughout the book, but are they the key themes? Or do the characters rise above the visual?

THE SHOEMAKER'S WIFE
By Adriana Trigiani

The majestic and haunting beauty of the Italian Alps is the setting of the first meeting of Enza, a practical beauty, and Ciro, a strapping mountain boy, who meet as teenagers, despite growing up in villages just a few miles apart. At the turn of the last century, when Ciro catches the local priest in a scandal, he is banished from his village and sent to hide in America as an apprentice to a shoemaker in Little Italy. Without explanation, he leaves a bereft Enza behind. Soon, Enza's family faces disaster and she, too, is forced to go to America with her father to secure their future.

Unbeknownst to one another, they both build fledgling lives in America, Ciro masters shoemaking and Enza takes a factory job in Hoboken until fate intervenes and reunites them. But it is too late…

"You don't need to have an immigrant family history to adore this novel— it ranks as one of Trigiani's very best. You only need a deep appreciation for exquisite writing and a story enriched by the power of abiding love." —**USA Today**

"I don't know how Adriana goes into her family's attic and emerges with these amazing stories, I'm just happy she does. If you're meeting her work for the first time, get ready for a lifelong love affair. The Shoemaker's Wife is utterly splendid." —**Kathryn Stockett, #1** *New York Times* **bestselling author**

ABOUT THE AUTHOR: **Adriana Trigiani** was raised in a small coal-mining town in southwest Virginia in a big Italian family. She chose her hometown for the setting and title of her debut novel, the critically acclaimed bestseller *Big Stone Gap*. The heartwarming story continues in the novel's sequels *Big Cherry Holler, Milk Glass Moon*, and *Home to Big Stone Gap*. Stand-alone novels *Lucia, Lucia; The Queen of the Big Time*; and *Rococo*, all topped the bestseller lists, as did Trigiani's 2009 *Very Valentine* and its 2010 sequel *Brava, Valentine*.

August 2012 | Trade Paperback | Fiction | 496 pp | $15.99 | ISBN 9780061257100
Harper Paperbacks | harpercollins.com | adrianatrigiani.com
Also available as: Audiobook, eBook, and large print

CONVERSATION STARTERS

1. The novel is split into three parts: Italian Alps, Manhattan and Minnesota. How would you characterize Ciro and Enza in each of these sections? How do they adapt to their new homes? In what ways did they change over the course of the novel? Enza and Ciro shared their first kiss beside Stella's grave. In what ways did digging the grave open up Ciro's heart?

2. When Ciro opened up his duffle bag on the ship to America, "the fragrance of the convent laundry—lavender and starch—enveloped him, fresh as the mountain air of Vilminore." What other aspects of convent life stayed with Ciro and Eduardo after they left? What did they learn from the sisters?

3. Enza "found a best friend in Laura, but so much more." What do you think made Laura and Enza's bond so deep from the beginning? In what ways did they support one another?

4. How does *The Shoemaker's Wife* portray the immigrant experience? Do any of your own families have a similar immigrant history? Did they have a different experience?

5. Enza and Ciro have different views of religion. In what ways do their beliefs shape their actions and relationship?

6. Carlo Lazzari warned Eduardo to "beware the things of this world that can mean everything or nothing." In what ways did this advice ring true throughout the novel?

7. When Ciro saw Enza on the steps of Our Lady of Pompeii church, moments away from marrying Vito, "it seemed like fate was on his side." Do you believe that fate brought Ciro and Enza together on that day? Overall, do you believe that Ciro and Enza were destined to be together?

8. Enza once said to Ciro: "I remind you, I imagine, of things you'd rather not think about." What do you believe Enza meant by this? What challenges did Ciro and Enza face in their relationship? How did they differ in their ways of communicating?

9. How did Ciro, Enza and Antonio each react to Ciro's diagnosis? What were Ciro's fears and hopes for his family? In what ways will Enza and Antonio fulfill his dreams?

10. At the end of the novel, Enza agrees to return to Italy with Antonio and Angela. How do you imagine the reunion between Enza and her family? How will Schilpario be different for Enza when seen through Angela and Antonio's eyes?

SHOUT HER LOVELY NAME
By Natalie Serber

Mothers and daughters ride the familial tide of joy, pride, regret, loathing, and love in these stories of resilient and flawed women. In a battle between a teenage daughter and her mother, wheat bread and plain yogurt become weapons. An aimless college student, married to her much older professor, sneaks cigarettes while caring for their newborn son. On the eve of her husband's fiftieth birthday, a pilfered fifth of rum, an unexpected tattoo, and rogue teenagers leave a woman questioning her place. And in a suite of stories, we follow capricious, ambitious single mother Ruby and her cautious, steadfast daughter Nora through their tumultuous life—stray men, stray cats, and psychedelic drugs—in 1970s California. Gimlet-eyed and emotionally generous, achingly real and beautifully written, these unforgettable stories lay bare the connection and conflict in families. *Shout Her Lovely Name* heralds the arrival of a powerful new writer.

"In the complexities of family triumphs and catastrophes, Natalie Serber is always achingly specific. Between mothers and daughters, women and their lovers, she misses nothing, and in all her scenes, the reader feels the true breath of life." —**Charles Baxter, author of *Gryphon***

"Call it fiction, but this collection is achingly true to life when it comes to the many ways mothers and daughters grow together and apart, over and over again." —**O, the Oprah Magazine**

ABOUT THE AUTHOR: **Natalie Serber** received an MFA from Warren Wilson College. Her work has appeared in The Bellingham Review and Gulf Coast, among others, and her awards include the Tobias Wolff Award. She teaches writing at various universities and lives with her family in Portland, Oregon. *Shout Her Lovely Name* is her debut book.

June 2012 | Hardcover | Fiction | 240 pp | $24.00 | ISBN 9780547634524
Houghton Mifflin Harcourt | hmhbooks.com | natalieserber.com
Also available as: eBook

CONVERSATION STARTERS

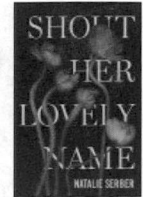

1. The first story in *Shout Her Lovely Name* deals with a mother trying to make sense of a disease that is tearing her family apart. Why do you think our society, when looking at eating and body image issues, tends to point to the mother as the responsible party? Or do you feel this may not be true? Why do the mother and father react differently to their daughter's disease?

2. In "Ruby Jewel," Ruby seems to have undergone changes during her time away at college that are evident to her family and the people in her town. Describe an experience in which you've felt removed from the community you grew up in.

3. Why do you think Ruby ignored her missed periods for so long? Do you think she was in denial or genuinely did not think that she was pregnant? Why do you think she engages in such reckless behavior after she finds out she's pregnant?

4. One of the other new mothers in the hospital tells Ruby, "Una hija will never leave you. Girls stick together." Do you think there is any truth to that statement? Are daughters more loyal to their mothers than sons?

5. The narrator of "This Is So Not Me" is married to a much older man. Do you think that it's possible to have an egalitarian relationship with a person who is significantly older than you?

6. In "A Whole Weekend of My Life," what do you think finally spurred Nora to see her father? Do you think Nora regrets reconnecting with her father? Do you think their relationship continued after their initial meeting?

7. Do you think it's possible for parents to have a relationship with their children after missing their childhood? Do you think it's better for parents to stay together for the sake of a child even if they aren't in love?

8. In the story "Rate My Life," Cassie seems to be experiencing some existential crisis in her life. What do you think set her on this path of ennui and discontent?

9. Many of the relationships portrayed throughout the collection are strained, and yet there is an undercurrent of love and desire to care for one another, hence the epigraph from Joni Mitchell. Do you think the stories are a fair representation of family life?

10. Some people think stories and novels about family and relationships are the territory of "women's" fiction. Do you agree that literature is gender-specific?

THE SOMETIMES DAUGHTER

Sherri Wood Emmons

Judy Webster is born in a mud-splattered tent at Woodstock, just as Crosby, Stills, and Nash take the stage. Her mother, Cassie, is a beautiful, flawed flower-child who brings her little girl to anti-war protests and parties rather than enroll her in pre-school. But as Cassie's husband, Kirk, gradually abandons '60s ideals in favor of a steady home and a law degree, their once idyllic marriage crumbles.

Dragging Judy back from the Kentucky commune where Cassie has taken her, Kirk files for divorce and is awarded custody. When Cassie eventually moves to an ashram in India, Judy is grief-stricken. At school, she constructs lies to explain her unconventional home-life, trying desperately to fit in to the world her mother rejected.

Cassie calls and writes, occasionally entering Judy's life just long enough to disrupt it. But little by little, Judy is growing up. As she grapples with her father's remarriage and her own reckless urges, she encounters all the joy and heartbreak that goes with first love, first loss, sex, drugs, and self-discovery. And when Cassie comes home again, Judy, who has tried so long to find a place in her mother's life, must finally decide what place Cassie claims in hers . . .

*"Emmons has a keen grasp of the difficulties of mother-daughter dynamics, and the specific struggles of young parents who are still figuring themselves out. She also paints the shifting turmoil of mid-'60s to early-'80s America with complexity, creating a vivid, expansive background for an intimate story." —***Publishers Weekly**

ABOUT THE AUTHOR: **Sherri Wood Emmons** is a freelance writer and editor. *Prayers and Lies* is her first work of fiction. She is a graduate of Earlham College and the University of Denver Publishing Institute. A mother of three, she lives in Indiana with her husband, two fat beagles, and four spoiled cats.

January 2012 | Trade Paperback | Fiction | 320 pp | $15.00 | ISBN 9780758253255
Kensington Books | kensingtonbooks.com | sherriwoodemmons.com
Also available as: eBook

CONVERSATION STARTERS

1. When Kirk decides to go to law school, Cassie accuses him of selling out his ideals for money. Is that an accurate assessment?

2. What role does Derrick play in the story? Does he bear any responsibility for the breakup of Cassie and Kirk's marriage?

3. What responsibility, if any, does Cassie's mother bear for her daughter's choices?

4. Is Kirk irresponsible for allowing Cassie to live with him when she returns from California?

5. After the Jonestown tragedy, Cassie continues to believe in Peoples Temple and Jim Jones. How can she hold on to those beliefs in the face of the mass suicides in Jonestown?

6. Why is Judy so angry with Cassie after their visit to Malibu? Is her behavior toward Cassie at Disneyland appropriate?

7. In Cassie's absence, Judy is mothered by three women—her grandmother, Lee Ann's mother, and Treva. Were there extra "mothers" in your life? What role did they play in making you who you are?

8. Is Matt's reaction to Judy after their arrest reasonable? Why can't he forgive Judy?

9. Why does Judy have sex with Patrick? Does this constitute rape?

10. Does Cassie's final revelation to Judy about her own teen pregnancy explain her behavior toward Judy and Kamran? Does it excuse her behavior?

SOUTH OF SUPERIOR
By Ellen Airgood

A debut novel full of heart, in which love, friendship, and charity teach a young woman to live a bigger life.

When Madeline Stone walks away from Chicago and moves five hundred miles north to the coast of Lake Superior, in Michigan's Upper Peninsula, she isn't prepared for how much her life will change.

Charged with caring for an aging family friend, Madeline finds herself in the middle of beautiful nowhere with Gladys and Arbutus, two octogenarian sisters—one sharp and stubborn, the other sweeter than sunshine. As Madeline begins to experience the ways of the small, tight-knit town, she is drawn into the lives and dramas of its residents. It's a place where times are tough and debts run deep, but friendship, community, and compassion run deeper. As the story hurtles along—featuring a lost child, a dashed love, a car accident, a wedding, a fire, and a romantic reunion—Gladys, Arbutus, and the rest of the town teach Madeline more about life, love, and goodwill than she's learned in a lifetime.

"Airgood's engaging debut is the novel, brimming with quirky characters, that everyone who moves to a small, tightly knit town imagines he or she might someday write." —Booklist

"Madeline Stone goes back to her roots in rural Michigan and finds the missing bits of herself, in a heartwarming . . . debut." —Kirkus Reviews

ABOUT THE AUTHOR: **Ellen Airgood** runs a diner in Grand Marais, Michigan. This is her first novel.

May 2012 | Trade Paperback | Fiction | 384 pp | $16.00 | ISBN 9781594485763
Riverhead | us.penguingroup.com | ellenairgood.com
Also available as: eBook

CONVERSATION STARTERS

1. Gladys always tells Madeline how much of an outsider she is, how much she doesn't understand the ways of McAllester. By the end of the novel do you think Madeline is a part of the town? In what ways has she let the community of McAllester transform her? In what way has she transformed the community?

2. Throughout the novel, Madeline is looking for a sense of purpose, for something to guide her life. At the end of the novel, do you think she's found that sense of purpose? What do you think it is?

3. Change is a major theme of the novel, and yet so much of what both Gladys and Madeline love about McAllester is how the town follows an older way of living. What kind of changes happen in the novel?

4. While Madeline and Gladys are deeply stubborn people, Arbutus is more likely to be adaptable. Do you think this makes Arbutus any less strong than the other women? In what ways is she just as stubborn? What do you think Madeline learns from Arbutus's way of getting what she wants?

5. Think about the Bensons. Do you think that they are wrong to want to improve their business? What could they have done to be more in keeping with the community? What does Madeline learn that they do not?

6. Values are important to all the characters in the novel. How are Madeline's values different from Gladys's? Paul's? What do you think Randi's values are? The Bensons's? Think about yourself. Which character do you feel most similar to?

7. At the start of the novel, Madeline takes an immediate dislike to Randi while Gladys has more patience for her. What do you think Gladys sees that Madeline does not? Think about how Madeline and Randi's relationship changes. How do you think Madeline's increased knowledge both about herself and about her history changes how she feels about Randi?

8. Life in McAllester is hard. Why do you think Madeline ultimately chooses it over returning to Chicago? What virtues do you see in it? What qualities would you want to emulate in your own life?

9. The novel ends on a note of anticipation. What do you think will happen to the characters after the book has ended? How do you think what Madeline has learned will help her handle future hardships?

STATE OF WONDER
By Ann Patchett

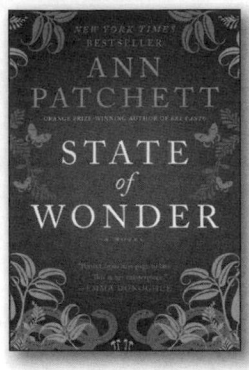

In a narrative replete with poison arrows, devouring snakes, scientific miracles, and spiritual transformations, *State of Wonder* presents a world of stunning surprise and danger, rich in emotional resonance and moral complexity.

As Dr. Marina Singh embarks upon an uncertain odyssey into the insect-infested Amazon, she will be forced to surrender herself to the lush but forbidding world that awaits within the jungle. Charged with finding her former mentor Dr. Annick Swenson, a researcher who has disappeared while working on a valuable new drug, she will have to confront her own memories of tragedy and sacrifice as she journeys into the unforgiving heart of darkness. Stirring and luminous, *State of Wonder* is a world unto itself, where unlikely beauty stands beside unimaginable loss beneath the rainforest's jeweled canopy.

"Emotionally lucid. . . . Patchett is at her lyrical best when she catalogues the jungle." —The New Yorker

"This is surely the smartest, most exciting novel of the summer." —***Washington Post***

ABOUT THE AUTHOR: **Ann Patchett** is the author of six novels: *State of Wonder*; *The New York Times* bestselling *Run*; *The Patron Saint of Liars*, which was a *New York Times* Notable Book of the Year; *Taft*, which won the Janet Heidinger Kafka Prize; *The Magician's Assistant*; and *Bel Canto*, which won the PEN/Faulkner Award, the Orange Prize, the BookSense Book of the Year, and was a finalist for the National Book Critics Circle Award. She is also the author of two works of nonfiction: *The New York Times* bestselling *Truth & Beauty* and *What now?* Patchett has written for many publications, including the *Atlantic Monthly, Harper's Magazine, Gourmet, The New York Times, Vogue*, and the *Washington Post*. She lives in Nashville, Tennessee.

May 2012 | Trade Paperback | Fiction | 384 pp | $15.99 | ISBN 9780062049810
Harper Perennial | harpercollins.com | annpatchett.com
Also available as: Audiobook, eBook, and large print

CONVERSATION STARTERS

1. How would you describe Marina Singh? How has the past shaped her character? Discuss the anxieties that are manifested in her dreams.
2. Consider Annik's research in the Amazon. Should women of any age be able to have children? What are the benefits and the downsides? Why does this ability seem to work in the Lakashi culture? What impact does this research ultimately have on Marina? Whether you are a man or woman, would you want to have a child in your fifties or sixties? How far should modern science go to "improve" on nature?
3. In talking about her experiences with the indigenous people, Annik explains, "the question is whether or not you choose to disturb the world around you; or if you choose to go on as if you had never arrived." How does Marina respond to this? Did Annik practice what she preached? How do these women's early choices impact later events and decisions? How does Annik's statement extend beyond the Amazon to the wider world? Would you rather make a "disturbance" in life, or go along quietly?
4. Talk about the Lakashi people and the researchers. How do they get along? Though the scientists try not to interfere with the natives' way of life, how does their being there impact the Lakashi? What influence do the Lakashi have on the scientists?
5. Marina travels into hell, into her own Conradian "heart of darkness." What keeps her in the jungle longer than she'd ever thought she'd stay? How does this journey transform her and her view of herself and the world? Will she ever return—and does she need to?
6. What is your opinion of the choices Marina made regarding Easter? What role did the boy play in the story? Do you think Marina will ever have the child—one like Easter—that she wants?
7. What do you think happens to Marina after she returns home?
8. *State of Wonder* is rich in symbolism. Identify a few—for example, Eden Prairie (Marina's Minnesota home), Easter (the young deaf native boy), Milton (the Brazilian guide)—and talk about how Ann Patchett uses them to deepen the story.
9. *State of Wonder* raises questions of morality and principle, civilization, culture, love, and science. Choose a few events from the book to explore some of these themes.
10. What is the significance of the novel's title, *State of Wonder*?

TERRORISTS IN LOVE
True Life Stories of Islamic Radicals

By Ken Ballen

Imagine a world where a boy's dreams dictate the behavior of warriors in battle; where a young couple's only release from forbidden love is death; where a suicide bomber survives only to become fiercely pro-American. This is the world of *Terrorists in Love*.

"An unusual atlas of extremism—a riveting, behind-the-scenes look at the events that turned six young Muslims into terrorists." —**Washington Post**

"[Ballen] adds nuance to a problem that Americans have tended to understand only in terms of good and evil . . . a much more human—though no less terrifying—picture of [those] committed to defeating the United States and Western civilization." —**The Boston Globe**

"More than a captivating read . . . exposing first-hand personal accounts . . . within the terrorist movement [that] likely will hasten its demise." —**Foreign Policy**

"One of the most in-depth looks at individual terrorists' lives currently available . . . helps reverse some major misconceptions about the motives of these attackers. Ultimately, in Terrorists in Love, *Ballen is bringing us closer to the real motives of terrorists, and thus closer to the truth. Even if that is uncomfortable, it's a step in the right direction."* —**The Huffington Post**

ABOUT THE AUTHOR: **Kenneth Ballen** is President and founder of Terror Free Tomorrow, a non-partisan, not-for-profit organization, which investigates the causes of extremism. As a federal prosecutor, Ballen successfully convicted international terrorists. He also prosecuted major figures in organized crime, international narcotics, and one of the first cases in the United States involving illegal financing for Middle Eastern terrorists. Ballen has regularly contributed to *CNN*, and its companion website CNN.com. His articles have also been published in the *Washington Post, Financial Times, Los Angeles Times, Foreign Policy, Wall Street Journal* and the *Christian Science Monitor*, among others.

June 2012 | Trade Paperback | Nonfiction | 336 pp | $15.00 | ISBN 9781451672589
Free Press | simonandschuster.com | terroristinlove.com
Also available as: eBook

CONVERSATION STARTERS

1. The title of the book is *Terrorists in Love*. How does love—or the lack of love—play a role in each of these stories? Why do you think Ballen gave the book this title?

2. Compare the different upbringings of the people profiled. What role does childhood play in forming these current and reformed terrorists? In your opinion, do formative moments of youth account for their commitment to jihad?

3. After reading these stories, how do you interpret radical jihad as it relates to orthodox Muslim practice? How are terrorist groups, like Al Qaeda and the Taliban, distorting the Quran's message, or following it?

4. Zeddy cites his mission to die for God as rooted in a "logic of emotion." How does emotion affect the six radicals' initial pledge to terror?

5. Of Malik, Mullah Omar's personal seer, Ballen writes: "He just wanted to do God's work. He had fought for jihad too but kept wondering who the real enemies of God were now." Why do you think his interactions with Pakistan's Inter-Services Intelligence (ISI) officers made him feel differently about his mission?

6. Some of the interviewees are murderers and terrorists. How do their accounts change your view of the Muslim radical? Did you feel any sympathy or compassion for any of the six individuals profiled? Can you "forgive" them, knowing what you now do about their struggles and paths?

7. Of Kamal, Ballen writes: "He now began to see that Al Qaeda's jihad fell short. Despite bin Laden's sacrifices, his jihad wasn't about finding the difficult struggle to better himself and others before God. Instead, Al Qaeda offered too much of a quick-and-easy path, a simple shortcut with ready-made answers that can lure someone from the long and hard true jihad of God." Do you think Kamal's view is correct?

8. How have these stories of ISI corruption influenced your view of Pakistan? Do you feel, as Zeddy suggests, that America is funding both sides of the war on terror?

9. The author poses the following question in the Afterword: "Without U.S. troops in Iraq, would Ahmad ever gone off to fight?" Discuss the role of American policy in fomenting radicalism as it relates to the radicals Ballen profiles in *Terrorists in Love*.

10. "Hope is as real as the hateful ideology of the terrorists." Do you agree? Explain your answer.

THOSE WE LOVE MOST
By Lee Woodruff

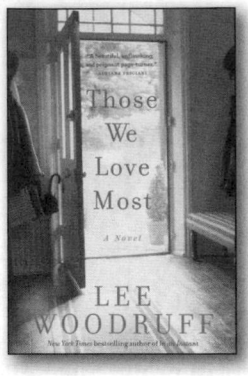

Life is good for Maura Corrigan. Married to her college sweetheart, Pete, raising three young kids with her parents nearby in her peaceful Chicago suburb, her world is secure. Then one day, in a single turn of fate, that entire world comes crashing down and everything that she thought she knew changes.

Maura must learn to move forward with the weight of grief and the crushing guilt of an unforgivable secret. Pete senses a gap growing between him and his wife but finds it easier to escape to the bar with his friends than face the flaws in his marriage.

Meanwhile, Maura's parents are dealing with the fault lines in their own marriage. Charismatic Roger, who at sixty-five, is still chasing the next business deal and Margaret, a pragmatic and proud homemaker, have been married for four decades, seemingly happily. But the truth is more complicated. Like Maura, Roger has secrets of his own and when his deceptions and weaknesses are exposed, Margaret's love and loyalty face the ultimate test.

"Lee Woodruff has written a beautiful, humorous, poignant page-turner about the complexities of love and marriage, tricky family dynamics, and the power of the human heart. Everything you want in a great read is here, including wonderful storytelling that builds to a satisfying ending. Loved it."
—**Adriana Trigiani**

About the Author: **Lee Woodruff** is the coauthor with her husband, Bob Woodruff, of the number one *New York Times* bestseller *In an Instant*, and the author of the essay collection *Perfectly Imperfect*. She is a contributing editor to CBS This Morning and has written numerous articles on family and parenting for *Parade, Ladies' Home Journal, Redbook, Country Living*, and *Family Fun*. Woodruff has four children and lives in Westchester County, New York.

September 2012 | Hardcover | Fiction | 320 pp | $26.99 | ISBN 9781401341787
Voice | hyperionbooks.com | leewoodruff.com
Also available as: eBook

CONVERSATION STARTERS

1. *Those We Love Most* has moments that are dark and painful. Why do you think Lee chose to write something that examines this side of life so intricately?
2. Lee has personal experience dealing with critically injured family members. Her husband, Bob, was struck by a roadside bomb in Iraq while reporting on the war, and he suffered extensive brain injuries and spent a year in speech and physical therapy. How much of Lee's life did you feel coming through in this story?
3. How guilty do you think Maura was in James's accident and death? Must some party always be guilty, even if their actions were unintended?
4. An ongoing theme in *Those We Love Most* is the ebb and flow of loving relationships and the changing currents of affection between people. How did James's death alter the currents of love between couples (both married and illicit)?
5. Lee writes that before James's death, Maura and Pete were "heading down that easy slipstream in marriage where the valuable, intimate parts begin to erode in a tidal wave of banality… How much love was enough love?" How much love do you think is enough in a marriage? Why do you think Maura and Pete's marriage survived James's death?
6. Do you think Alex will be able to overcome the trauma of killing James? Was going into the military a good choice for Alex?
7. Margaret's characterization as a stoic, firm, emotionally controlled matriarch is written with reverence and respect. Do you agree with Margaret's emotional choices? What flaws, if any, did you find with Lee's characterization of Margaret?
8. How did Roger's stroke alter the trajectories of the central relationships in the book? What were the positive effects, if any, of the stroke?
9. How do you think the book's central relationships would have played out differently if James had survived the accident? Consider the triangles of Maura, Pete and Art, and Roger, Julia and Margaret.
10. Toward the end of the book, Margaret thinks, "It was times like this you understood what you had; you could take an accounting in a way you weren't able to when life ran smoothly." Do you think people need to go through hard times in order to appreciate other aspect of life and family?
11. How were Roger and Maura's motivations to be unfaithful and their entanglements the same or different?

TIES THAT BIND
A Cobbled Court Novel
Marie Bostwick

Christmas is fast approaching, and New Bern, Connecticut, is about to receive the gift of a new pastor, hired sight unseen to fill in while Reverend Tucker is on sabbatical. Meanwhile, Margot Matthews' friend, Abigail, is trying to matchmake even though Margot has all but given up on romance. She loves her job at the Cobbled Court Quilt Shop and the life and friendships she's made in New Bern; she just never thought she'd still be single on her fortieth birthday.

It's a shock to the entire town when Phillip A. Clarkson turns out to be Philippa. Truth be told, not everyone is happy about having a female pastor. Yet despite a rocky start, Philippa begins to settle in—finding ways to ease the townspeople's burdens, joining the quilting circle, and forging a fast friendship with Margot. When tragedy threatens to tear Margot's family apart, that bond—and the help of her quilting sisterhood—will prove a saving grace. And as she untangles her feelings for another new arrival in town, Margot begins to realize that it is the surprising detours woven into life's fabric that provide its richest hues and deepest meaning . . .

"This is one very talented writer . . . watch her star rise!" —**Debbie Macomber, author of Three Wishes**

"The beautiful prose in this multilayered faith and community based novel gives life to a small New England town filled with characters readers will long remember." —**RT Book Reviews, 4.5 Stars, Top Pick**

About the Author: **Marie Bostwick** was born and raised in the Northwest. Since marrying the love of her life many years ago, she and her family have moved a score of times, living in eight US states and two Mexican cities, and collecting a vast and cherished array of friends and experiences. Marie now lives with her husband in Connecticut where she writes, reads, quilts, and is active in her local church.

May 2012 | Trade Paperback | Fiction | 368 pp | $15.00 | ISBN 9780758269287
Kensington Books | kensingtonbooks.com | mariebostwick.com
Also available as: eBook and Audiobook

CONVERSATION STARTERS

1. We all know that there's no such thing as a perfect family, and Margot's is no exception. What did your parents do right? What do you wish they'd done differently? If you're a parent, how did your childhood experiences shape the way you raised or are raising your children?

2. Philippa had a number of careers before finally responding to the call to ministry. Why do you think it took her so long to do so? Have you ever changed career paths? Tell the group about your experiences. What was difficult about it? What was easier than you thought it would be? If you could do it over again, would you? And if you've never changed careers, do you wish you could?

3. People deal with grief and loss in very different ways. Margot, her parents, her niece, and Philippa have each undergone a terrible loss at some point in their lives. How did their responses to grief differ? How were they similar? What does the manner in which they respond to loss say about their personalities? If you have ever grieved the loss of someone close to you, how did you get through it?

4. Margot has had many male friends in her lifetime, yet those friendships never seem to blossom into romance. Why do you suppose that is? Do you think that all those men were truly uninterested in Margot romantically? Could she have been sending out unconscious signals that she wasn't interested in them?

5. Margot often says that she's given up looking for "Mr. Right" and would happily settle for "Mr. Good Enough," but do you think that's true? How might Margot's views about sex outside of marriage have affected her relationships with men?

6. Philippa and Margot both want children but, for different reasons, face obstacles to realizing that dream. Have you, or has someone you know, been faced with issues of infertility? What about life as a single parent? Do you think it is important for children to be raised in a two-parent home?

7. When Margot first meets Paul, she could not find him less appealing. However, as the story progresses, her feelings toward him move from disinterest to friendship to true love. Do you think this is the usual way for romantic attachments to develop? Or do you believe in love at first sight? What about your story?

THE TIME KEEPER

By Mitch Albom

In Mitch Albom's newest work of fiction, the inventor of the world's first clock is punished for trying to measure God's greatest gift. He is banished to a cave for centuries and forced to listen to the voices of all who come after him seeking more days, more years. Eventually, with his soul nearly broken, Father Time is granted his freedom, along with a magical hourglass and a mission: a chance to redeem himself by teaching two earthly people the true meaning of time.

He returns to our world—now dominated by the hour-counting he so innocently began—and commences a journey with two unlikely partners: one a teenage girl who is about to give up on life, the other a wealthy old businessman who wants to live forever. To save himself, he must save them both. And stop the world to do so.

Told in Albom's signature spare, evocative prose, this remarkably original tale will inspire readers everywhere to reconsider their own notions of time, how they spend it and how precious it truly is.

"Think of Mitch Albom as the Babe Ruth of popular literature, hitting the ball out of the park every time he's at bat." —TIME **Magazine**

"One of my favorite writers: a fearless explorer of the wishful and magical." —**James McBride**

ABOUT THE AUTHOR: **Mitch Albom** is an author, playwright, and screenwriter who has written seven books, including the international bestseller *Tuesdays with Morrie*, the bestselling memoir of all time. His first novel, *The Five People You Meet in Heaven*, was an instant #1 *New York Times* bestseller, as were *For One More Day*, his second novel, and *Have a Little Faith*, his most recent work of nonfiction. All four books were made into acclaimed TV films. Albom also works as a columnist and a broadcaster and has founded seven charities in Detroit and Haiti, where he operates an orphanage/mission. He lives with his wife, Janine, in Michigan.

September 2012 | Hardcover | Fiction | 240 pp | $24.99 | ISBN 9781401322786
Hyperion | hyperionbooks.com | mitchalbom.com
Also available as: eBook and Audiobook

CONVERSATION STARTERS

1. In what ways were you aware of the role time plays in your life before you read *The Time Keeper*? Besides watching the clock, make a list of ways you count or measure in your everyday life. Explore the many ways that measuring and counting have benefitted human beings in the history of our development.

2. Considering Dor's eventual obsession with measurements of time, what are the dangers of such an approach to life? Where do you draw the line for yourself?

3. Think about Dor's final visit with King Nim. What makes Nim a leader of the people? Are his and Dor's abilities mutually exclusive? Why does Dor refuse to help Nim? Why must Nim banish Dor from the kingdom?

4. Chapter 36 begins with the question "Can you imagine having endless time to learn?" Would you want time to be endless? Why or why not?

5. Consider Sarah Lemon. What is she like? What are her particular, significant challenges in the world?

6. When we first meet Sarah, she is begging for more time as she gets ready for her date with Ethan. Much later, she desperately wants time to just end. How do you explain such profound differences in her attitude toward time?

7. What is Victor Delamonte like? In what ways has his disciplined work ethic benefitted him? In what ways has it limited his life experience?

8. Both Sarah and Victor act with desperation regarding their time due to profound suffering. Is this always the case, that it is only when things are not well that time seems slower?

9. From Sarah, Dor learns the phrase *time flies* (when you're having fun). Why does time seem to go faster when we enjoy ourselves? Is this always the case?

10. During his torturous time in the cave, Dor makes symbols on the wall to mark and remember key moments in his life. What are the many ways we mark the passing of time? How—other than by taking photos—do you order and stay connected to times past?

11. Albom uses the technique of showing characters the future. What other examples of this in literature can you think of?

12. What's the significance of Victor choosing his wife's name, Grace, as the emergency word to stop the cryonics process?

A TRAIN IN THE WINTER

The Extraordinary Story of Women, Friendship, and Resistance in Occupied France

By Caroline Moorehead

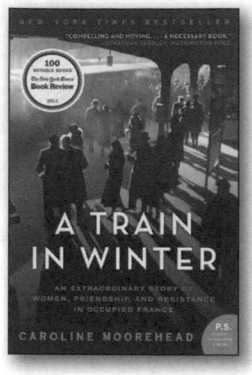

In January 1943, 230 women of the French Resistance were sent to the death camps by the Nazis who had invaded and occupied their country. This is their story, told in full for the first time—a searing and unforgettable chronicle of terror, courage, defiance, survival, and the power of friendship. Caroline Moorehead, a distinguished biographer, human rights journalist, and the author of *Dancing to the Precipice* and *Human Cargo*, brings to life an extraordinary story that readers of Mitchell Zuckoff's *Lost in Shangri-La*, Erik Larson's *In the Garden of Beasts*, and Laura Hillenbrand's *Unbroken* will find an essential addition to our retelling of the history of World War II—a riveting, rediscovered story of courageous women who sacrificed everything to combat the march of evil across the world.

"By turns heartbreaking and inspiring." —**Caroline Weber, *The New York Times Book Review***

"[Moorehead] traces the lives and deaths of all her subjects with unswerving candor and compassion. . . . In Moorehead's telling, neither evil nor good is banal; and if the latter doesn't always triumph, it certainly inspires." —*USA Today*

About the Author: **Caroline Moorehead** is the biographer of Bertrand Russell, Freya Stark, Iris Origo, and Martha Gellhorn. Well known for her work in human rights, she has published a history of the Red Cross and an acclaimed book about refugees, *Human Cargo*. Her previous book was *Dancing to the Precipice*, a biography of Lucie de la Tour du Pin. She lives in London and Italy.

October 2012 | Trade Paperback | Fiction | 400 pp | $15.99 | ISBN 9780061650710
Harper Perennial | harpercollins.com
Also available as: eBook and large print

CONVERSATION STARTERS

1. What is the importance of women's friendship in *A Train in Winter*? How is it shown, what forms does it take, and what difference does it make to the lives of the women described in the book?

2. How has this book changed your view of World War II, the French Resistance, the role of women in wartime, the Holocaust, or another subject discussed in the book?

3. Caroline Moorehead takes care in the book to tell individual stories. Which of these had the greatest impact on you while reading the book, and why?

4. What motives for the women's resistance work are presented in *A Train in Winter*? Are their reasons the same as those of men?

5. What will you remember about *A Train in Winter*?

6. If you could ask one of the survivors of the Convoi des 31000 a question about her experiences, what would it be?

7. Why do you think the history discussed in *A Train in Winter* was buried for so long?

8. What do you think was behind "attentisme"—holding on, waiting, doing nothing—the initial French reaction to the Occupation?

9. The women of the Convoi des 31000 longed to come home from the camps—but then those few who did so found their return to be sometimes impossibly hard. Why was this the case?

10. What lessons should we learn from *A Train in Winter*?

11. What role did the Communist Party play in the French Resistance? How were perspectives on it altered, first by the Nazi-Soviet Non-Aggression Pact, and then by the German invasion of the Soviet Union?

12. Debate the issue of French collaboration with the Nazi authorities as it is described in the book. What do you think you would do if you were placed in some of the situations Caroline Moorehead describes?

13. What do you make of the turn in recent historical writing to "microhistories" of individual moments and stories, rather than grand abstract narratives? Which kind of historical writing do you prefer, and why?

14. If you could invite Caroline Moorehead to your book club discussion, what would you like to ask her about *A Train in Winter*, and why?

THE VANISHING ACT
By Mette Jakobsen

On a small snow-covered island—so tiny that it can't be found on any map—lives twelve-year-old Minou, her philosopher Papa (a descendant of Descartes), Boxman the magician, and a clever dog called No-Name. A year earlier Minou's mother left the house wearing her best shoes and carrying a large black umbrella. She never returned.

One morning Minou finds a dead boy washed up on the beach. Her father decides to lay him in the room that once belonged to her mother. Can her mother's disappearance be explained by the boy? Will Boxman be able to help find her? Minou, unwilling to accept her mother's death, attempts to find the truth through Descartes' philosophy. Over the course of her investigation Minou will discover the truth about loss and love, a truth that *The Vanishing Act* conveys in a voice that is uniquely enchanting.

"The best stories change you. I am not the same after The Vanishing Act *as I was before."* —**Erin Morgenstern, author of *The Night Circus***

ABOUT THE AUTHOR: **Mette Jakobsen** was born in Denmark in 1964. She holds degrees in philosophy and creative writing and is the author of several plays. *The Vanishing Act* is her first novel. She lives in Sydney, Australia.

September 2012 | Hardcover | Fiction | 208 pp | $23.95 | ISBN 9780393062922
W. W. Norton and Co. | wwnorton.com
Also available as: eBook

CONVERSATION STARTERS

1. Each of the characters has a personal philosophy that colors how they view what happens in their lives. How do those philosophies explain who each of them is?

2. Why does the author choose as her title *The Vanishing Act*?

3. At the beginning of the story, Minou and her father find a dead boy. How does his presence help Minou and her father? How does he come to mean more to them than an unknown person?

4. Discuss the setting of the island. Why did the author decide to set her novel there?

5. Mama and Papa had different experiences during the war. What effects did their lives at that time have on them?

6. What is the significance of the lighthouse? Why does Papa keep the light off?

7. Minou's grandfather sends many postcards to Papa. What message is the grandfather sending Papa and why does he send ones exclusively with the same art?

8. Theodora is the founder of the island and has become a legend for the people who live there. How does her story affect each of the characters?

9. Why did Mama disappear? What happened to her?

10. Are reason and magic compatible? How does Minou integrate both in her life?

THE WATCH

By Joydeep Roy-Bhattacharya

Following a desperate night-long battle, a group of beleaguered soldiers in an isolated base in Kandahar are faced with a lone woman demanding the return of her brother's body. Is she a spy, a black widow, a lunatic, or is she what she claims to be: a grieving young sister intent on burying her brother according to local rites? Single-minded in her mission, she refuses to move from her spot on the field in full view of every soldier in the stark outpost. Her presence quickly proves dangerous as the camp's tense, claustrophobic atmosphere comes to a boil when the men begin arguing about what to do next.

Joydeep Roy-Bhattacharya's heartbreaking and haunting novel, *The Watch*, takes a timeless tragedy and hurls it into present-day Afghanistan. Taking its cues from the *Antigone* myth, Roy-Bhattacharya brilliantly recreates the chaos, intensity, and immediacy of battle, and conveys the inevitable repercussions felt by the soldiers, their families, and by one sister. The result is a gripping tour through the reality of this very contemporary conflict, and our most powerful expression to date of the nature and futility of war.

"Roy-Bhattacharya re-animates the timeless themes of Antigone. . . . *This brave, visceral novel breaks new ground and does what previous versions of* Antigone *never have: It makes each character deeply humane, challenging the reader to sympathize with every one of them."* —**NPR.org**

"We watch as the resistance of an isolated American garrison in Afghanistan is ground down, not by force of arms but by the will of a single unarmed woman, holding inflexibly to an idea of what is just and right." —**J.M. Coetzee, recipient of the Nobel Prize and a two-time Man Booker Prize winner**

ABOUT THE AUTHOR: **Joydeep Roy-Bhattacharya** was educated in politics and philosophy at Presidency College, Calcutta, and the University of Pennsylvania. His novels *The Gabriel Club* and *The Storyteller of Marrakesh* have been published in fourteen languages. He lives in the Hudson Valley in upstate New York.

June 2012 | Hardcover | Fiction | 304 pp | $25.00 | ISBN 9780307955890
Paperback available May 2013 (ISBN 9780307955913; $15.00)
Hogarth | randomhouse.com | joydeeproybhattacharya.com
Also available as: eBook and Audiobook

CONVERSATION STARTERS

1. What were your initial theories about Nizam? How did your opinion of her, and of the U.S. soldiers, shift throughout the novel?

2. As with Antigone's brother, the guilt or innocence of Nizam's brother makes for a provocative debate. The motivations of Nizam's brother are probed in-depth in "Captain," at 0545, a scene in which Tanner asks, "Will someone please tell me who the good guys are?" What's the best answer to his question?

3. In "Lieutenant" and "Lieutenant's Journal," we see Nick Frobenius struggle with his memories of home, particularly his relationship with his former wife, Emily. What is at the heart of his struggle? How does his story capture the chasm between a tour of duty and the requirements of civilian life?

4. As Second Lieutenant Tom Ellison recalls his father, what dialogues about America's involvement in Afghanistan overall is he bringing to light? Did you side with Tom or with his father in those discussions?

5. How did First Sergeant Jimmy Whalen's aunt help to strengthen his psyche? On page 196, what do we discover about his leadership style as he listens to the description of Pratt's disturbing dream (which echoes a premonition in the *Antigone* saga)?

6. As you witnessed the chain of command within each chapter, what did you notice about the characters' use of authority? What distinctions did you observe between officers and enlisted men?

7. Ultimately, what leads to the transformation of Captain Evan Connolly (whom Masood calls "Comandan Saab")? How would you respond to the question Masood asks the captain in the closing lines of the book? What broader answers about war can be delivered in response to the "Why?" of Masood?

8. Re-read passages from the first chapter. What does this exercise reveal about perception and interpretation, from the word "wire" to the soldiers' attempts to protect Nizam?

9. Before reading *The Watch,* how deep was your understanding of Afghanistan's history? What can a novel reveal about history that a memoir or history book cannot?

10. The coda is spoken by Creon in Sophocles' play *Antigone.* In that scene, Creon is justifying his actions to his son, who is in love with Antigone. What are your reactions to Creon's defense? How does it resonate in global politics today?

A WORLD WITHOUT CANCER

The Making of a New Cure and the Real Promise of Prevention

By Margaret I. Cuomo, MD

A provocative and surprising investigation into the ways that profit, personalities, and politics obstruct real progress in the war on cancer—and one doctor's passionate call to action for change.

As a diagnostic radiologist who has watched patients, friends, and family suffer with and die from cancer and who was deeply affected by the enraged husband of one patient, Dr. Margaret I. Cuomo is inspired to seek out new strategies for waging a smarter war on cancer.

This year, about 1.6 million new cases of cancer will be diagnosed and more than 1,500 people will die per day. We've been asked to accept the disappointing strategy to "manage cancer as a chronic disease." We've allowed pharmaceutical companies to position cancer drugs that extend life by just weeks and may cost $100,000 for a single course of treatment as breakthroughs. Where is the bold leadership that will transform our system from treatment to prevention? Have we forgotten the mission of the National Cancer Act of 1971 to "conquer cancer"?

Through an analysis of more than 40 years of medical evidence and interviews with the top cancer researchers, drug company executives, and health policy advisers, Dr. Cuomo reveals intriguing answers to these questions. She shows us how all cancer stakeholders—the pharmaceutical industry, the government, physicians, and concerned Americans—can change the way we view and fight cancer in this country.

ABOUT THE AUTHOR: **Margaret I. Cuomo, MD**, is a board-certified radiologist who served as an attending physician in diagnostic radiology at North Shore University Hospital in Manhasset, New York, for many years. Specializing in body imaging, involving CT, ultrasound, MRI, and interventional procedures, much of her practice was dedicated to the diagnosis of cancer and AIDS. She is the daughter of former New York Governor Mario Cuomo and Mrs. Matilda Cuomo and sister to Governor Andrew Cuomo and ABC's Chris Cuomo. She resides in New York.

October 2012 | Hardcover | Nonfiction | 288 pp | $26.99 | ISBN 978160961885
Rodale | rodaleinc.com
Also available as: eBook

CONVERSATION STARTERS

1. In the introduction, Dr. Cuomo tells a story about breaking the news to a patient that her cancer may have returned and explores how difficult both delivering that news and hearing it can be. Have you or someone you loved had a cancer scare or received a cancer diagnosis? How compassionately or professionally did the doctor deliver the news?

2. Why do you think some people avoid cancer screenings? Are they fearful that something might be wrong? Are they just too busy? Do you think that cancer screenings actually save lives?

3. What could be some of the reasons why cancer treatments have grown more and more expensive and yet not become any more effective? Is there any way to improve their effectiveness and keep costs under control?

4. When you think of "dealing" with cancer, the focus is often on the treatment. But Toni and Doug's story in Chapter 7 reminds us of many factors, costs, and strains patients and their families must cope with. Can you put yourself in Toni's place? How would you balance the desire to live with the agony of the treatments?

5. Health care has become a major political and social issue. What is problematic about the way healthcare is approached in the United States? What do you think are the consequences of accepting cancer as an impossible-to-defeat inevitability, treating it as a chronic disease rather than trying to prevent or eliminate it?

6. Why do you think, that despite the decades of grave warnings we've been given about tobacco, almost 20% of the adult population still smokes? What can be done to reduce this statistic? Do you think that the medical community and government have done enough to help end smoking?

7. What are some specific ways that the government can encourage healthier living? How can new 21st-century technologies play a role? To what extent do you believe the government should guide or intervene in the health choices of citizens? Should schools play a greater role in teaching our children about healthier lifestyles?

8. Dr. Cuomo reports on research that shows we could prevent 50 percent of all cancers with the information we have right now. Then she outlines the ways in Chapters 10–13. What are the steps that are hardest for you to follow and why? What have you learned from this book that you will apply to your own life?

THE YEAR OF THE GADFLY

By Jennifer Miller

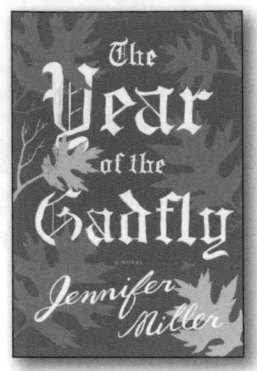

Storied, fiercely competitive Mariana Academy was founded with a serious honor code; its reputation has been unsullied for decades. Now a long-dormant secret society, Prisom's Party, threatens its placid halls with vigilante justice, exposing students and teachers alike for even the most minor infraction.

Iris Dupont, a budding journalist whose only confidant is the chain-smoking specter of Edward R. Murrow, feels sure she can break into the ranks of *The Devil's Advocate*, the Party's underground newspaper, and there uncover the source of its blackmail schemes and vilifying rumors. Some involve the school's new science teacher, who also seems to be investigating the Party. Others point to an albino student who left school abruptly ten years before, never to return. And everything connects to a rare book called *Marvelous Species*. But the truth comes with its own dangers, and Iris is torn between her allegiances, her reporter's instinct, and her own troubled past.

The Year of the Gadfly is an exhilarating journey of double-crosses, deeply buried secrets, and the lifelong reverberations of losing someone you love. Following in the tradition of classic school novels such as *A Separate Peace*, *Prep*, and *The Secret History*, it reminds us how these years haunt our lives forever.

"A darkly comic romp . . . vivid and very enjoyable." —The Washington Post

ABOUT THE AUTHOR: **Jennifer Miller**, the author of *Inheriting the Holy Land: An American's Search for Hope in the Middle East*, holds a BA from Brown University, an MS in Journalism from Columbia, and an MFA in fiction writing at Columbia. Her work has been published in *The New York Times, Marie Claire, Men's Health*, the *Christian Science Monitor*, Salon.com, and others. She is a native of Washington, D.C., and currently lives in Brooklyn with all the other writers.

May 2012 | Hardcover | 384 pp | $24.00 | ISBN 9780547548593
Houghton Mifflin Harcourt | hmhbooks.com | byjennifermiller.com
Also available as: eBook

CONVERSATION STARTERS

1. In the beginning of the novel the author uses phrases like, "The seat belt held me like a straitjacket," and "The place screamed asylum more than school." She also describes the houses in Nye as "in various stages of decay and abandonment." What kind of mood did these images create for the opening scenes?

2. In addition to speaking to the specter of Murrow, Iris spends time imagining the lives of Lily, the schoolgirl whose room she uses, and her deceased friend, Dalia. What do you think this focus tells us about her worldview? What does it tell you about Iris as a character and her development over the course of the novel?

3. Hazel, the Nye Historical Society's curator, talks with Iris about Socrates and his role as a gadfly. Iris considers herself a gadfly. What does she mean? What were Hazel's motivations in bringing it up?

4. Iris is kidnapped by four students in pig masks. One tells her, "Just because something looks sinister doesn't mean it is." How does Iris relate this to Kaplan's theories and to the *Marvelous Species* manuscript on microorganisms? How does she relate this concept to life itself?

5. Iris recalls Mr. Kaplan saying, "With all the dead skin cells and falling leaves, the world is dying as much as it's living." Is there a positive and negative way to view this kind of process?

6. Jonah Kaplan says, "We all desired what we could not have. Justin, Lily, and myself. Even Hazel." How does each character desire what could not be attained? Does that apply to Iris as well? Why or why not? Is unrequited and unquenched desire something that seems especially true in adolescence?

7. At one point the imaginary Ed Murrow says to Iris, "There is no Edward R. Murrow. There's only the myth of him." What did he mean by this? How does this change Iris? Why do you think Iris has Edward Murrow as an imaginary friend and role model? What might have prompted the author to choose him for this role?

8. "Most good things in life come prepackaged with nostalgia; otherwise nobody would appreciate anything." Do you agree or disagree? How do we overcome our pasts, or, why and how do the characters in this book struggle to shed their pasts? Do they succeed? Can anyone? Would you want to succeed at such a goal?

A MUST-READ FOR YOUR BOOK CLUB

National Book Award Winner

◇◇◇◇◇◇◇◇◇◇◇◇◇◇◇◇◇◇◇◇◇◇◇◇◇◇◇◇

Hurricane Katrina threatens the town of Bois Sauvage, Mississippi, and Esch's father can feel it in his bones. Esch, fifteen and motherless, has just realized she's pregnant, and together with her three brothers and father, she will face the coming storm and the day that will dawn after.

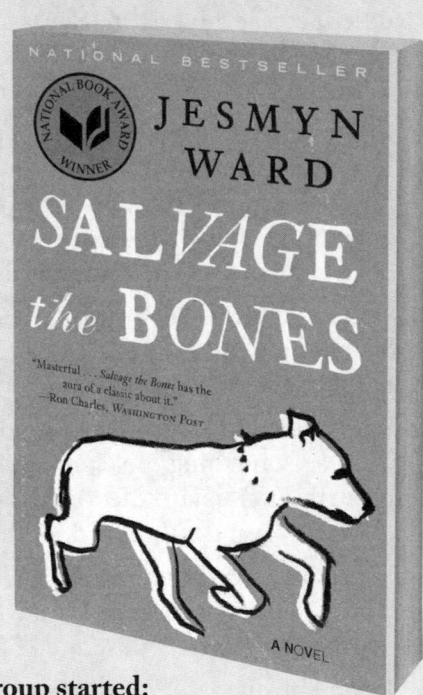

Some questions to get your group started:

• *Salvage the Bones* opens with China giving birth to a litter of puppies in the shed. What do we learn about Esch and the rest of the Batiste family during this scene?

• Esch's summer reading assignment, *Mythology* by Edith Hamilton, includes the story of the tragic romance between Jason and Medea. In the end, does Esch betray her family for love, as Medea did?

• Discuss the setting of *Salvage the Bones*. How does the Pit—the lot where the Batiste family has lived for generations—look and feel? What is it like to grow up in the town of Bois Sauvage?

Visit www.bloomsbury.com for more discussion questions.

Available wherever books are sold.

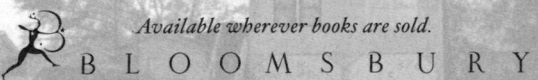

B L O O M S B U R Y

Four girls. Four mothers. One unforgettable summer.

JULIE SCHUMACHER

The Unbearable Book Club for Unsinkable Girls

At the start of summer Adrienne, CeeCee, Jill, and Wallis were not friends. But as literary prisoners of a mother-daughter book club, they navigate the classics and unexpected catastrophes to discover that the best stories have no endings.

Read & Discuss

- Why do you think the mothers wanted to create a book club for their daughters? What were their motives?

- Which character do you relate to the most and why?

- Adrienne opens each chapter of the book with a literary term. Which one was your favorite? Why?

- All the books read in the book club have female protagonists. Why do you think that is?

Read an excerpt at RandomBuzzers.com

 RHCB Delacorte Press

extremely witty conversation with southern authors
most excellent recommendations for reading
clever & refined musings of booksellers & writers
engaging & amusing author readings
illuminating excerpts from great southern books
and other such items as are of interest to
her ladyship, the editor

Lady Banks' Commonplace Book

front porch literary gossip
from your favorite southern bookshops

subscribe at ladybankscommonplacebook.com